THE
HOUSE
BOOK

THE
HOUSE
BOOK

INCLUDES MORE THAN 250 INSTANT DECORATING IDEAS, WITH OVER 2000 PHOTOGRAPHS AND ILLUSTRATIONS

MIKE LAWRENCE
with Stewart and
Sally Walton

HERMES
HOUSE

This edition is published by Hermes House,
an imprint of
Anness Publishing Ltd
Hermes House
88–89 Blackfriars Road
London SE1 8HA
tel. 020 7401 2077; fax 020 7633 9499
www.hermeshouse.com;
www.annesspublishing.com

If you like the images in this book and would like
to investigate using them for publishing, promo-
tions or advertising, please visit our website
www.practicalpictures.com for more information.

Publisher Joanna Lorenz
Editorial Director Judith Simons
Project Editor Katy Bevan
Photography John Freeman, Graham Rae
Designers Michael Morey, Simon Wilder
Additional Contributions Jan Eaton, Catherine
Tully, Judy Smith, Andrea Spencer, Diana Civil

ETHICAL TRADING POLICY
At Anness Publishing we believe that business
should be conducted in an ethical and ecologically
sustainable way, with respect for the environment
and a proper regard to the replacement of the
natural resources we employ.
As a publisher, we use a lot of wood pulp to make
high-quality paper for printing, and that wood
commonly comes from spruce trees. We are
therefore currently growing more than 750,000
trees in three Scottish forest plantations:
Berrymoss (130 hectares/320 acres), West Touxhill
(125 hectares/305 acres) and Deveron Forest
(75 hectares/185 acres). The forests we manage
contain more than 3.5 times the number of trees
employed each year in making paper for the books
we manufacture.
Because of this ongoing ecological investment
programme, you, as our customer, can have the
pleasure and reassurance of knowing that a tree is
being cultivated on your behalf to naturally
replace the materials used to make the book you
are holding.
Our forestry programme is run in accordance with
the UK Woodland Assurance Scheme (UKWAS)
and will be certified by the internationally recog-
nized Forest Stewardship Council (FSC). The FSC
is a non-government organization dedicated to
promoting responsible management of the world's
forests. Certification ensures forests are managed
in an environmentally sustainable and socially
responsible way. For further information about this
scheme, go to www.annesspublishing.com/trees

Previously published as *The Ultimate Book of
Decorating and Do-It-Yourself*

PUBLISHER'S NOTE
Although the advice and information in this
book are believed to be accurate and true at the
time of going to press, neither the authors nor
the publisher can accept any legal responsibility
or liability for any errors or omissions that may
be made nor for any inaccuracies nor for any
harm or injury that comes about from following
instructions or advice in this book.

CONTENTS

ABOUT THIS BOOK

Home improvement has never been as popular as it is today. For a start, there are more homeowners than ever before, according to the latest statistics, and the majority of them want their homes to look attractive, to feature the latest furnishings and decorations, and to have a sense of style that reflects their personalities.

The media also has home improvement high on the agenda. Terrestrial, satellite and cable TV channels offer an ever-increasing variety of do-it-yourself and home improvement programmes, covering every aspect of the subject from demolition to decoration – and creating a new stable of celebrity

designers in the process. The newsagents' stands are filled with home interest magazines, which give guidance on creating every home style imaginable from period living and country cottage to modern minimalism.

Books deal with every practical topic, from do-it-yourself basics to self-building, and also offer style and interior design advice to suit every taste. The degree of choice available is almost overwhelming, and making clear decisions about what to import

into the home becomes increasingly difficult as a result. Venture
into the home improvement superstores, and there are more
choices to be made. Which type of paint? What colour? How about new
wallpaper, or tiles, or flooring? What kind of bathroom and kitchen equipment should you
choose? And what about light fittings, soft furnishings, or shelves and storage solutions? It
is hard to know where to start… but help is at hand.

This book is designed to simplify the decorating and home improvement
challenge. It takes the reader through a process of analysis,
treating the existing home as a blank canvas and
making it easier to assess precisely what is required to
achieve a particular end result. It
looks in detail at every aspect of ➤

every room in the house, offering advice on choosing and using a varied range of decoration, features, fittings and furnishings to give each room its own sense of style and unity.

The second half of the book presents a range of creative makeover ideas. These are quick and easy projects that can be completed in a weekend, so they are ideal for busy working people, allowing you to achieve lasting results with the minimum of time and effort. This section is divided into six chapters. Windows show you how to transform your home with

modern fixtures and fittings, quick drapes and stylish tie-backs. The chapter on Walls and Floors demonstrates original decorating ideas that will give your home a visual lift, from original wall hangings and fabulous rugs to panelled walls and stencilled flooring designs. Beds and Bedding gives you step-by-step instructions for revamping your bedroom from fabulous cushions and pillows to decorative headboard ideas.

Chairs and Tables looks at decorating furniture, Light and Shade gives ideas for updating and making new lighting arrangements, and Containers has creative storage ideas to keep your home and work station tidy.

The emphasis throughout is on combining style and practicality, so that every job can be approached confidently from planning to execution. With clear instructions and detailed step-by-step photography, everything is eminently achievable.

The information provided aims to help everyone, from the absolute beginner to the more practised homeowner, to achieve sensational results by getting things right from the very start, with no wasted effort or money. It is a source book for every aspect of decorating and styling the home, and it will guide the reader unerringly from concept to completion time after time.

PART ONE
PRACTICAL DECORATING

INTRODUCTION

The interior of a home is like a giant mirror, reflecting the owners' character, taste, aspirations and interests – even their little foibles. The purpose of this book is to help in making decisions that will create a home that reflects the personality of the owners, and one that they are happy to live in. It starts by explaining how to examine the present state of things, and to work out what should be retained and what would be better changed. This first chapter assesses the benefits of some basic internal alterations, such as reorganizing the use of space or how the furniture is arranged, and goes on to plan new decorating and furnishing schemes in conjunction with another very important but often overlooked factor: lighting. The next stage is to plan in in detail how to carry out work in a well-organized and strictly methodical way, which is vital to success.

The rest of part one contains chapters that deal with every type of home improvement task, from the use of paint, wall coverings, tiles and floor coverings to features and fittings, soft furnishings and storage, and it closes with a look at the routine maintenance and repair jobs that every householder has to face from time to time. Each chapter gives full information on the tools and materials that will be used, and covers a wide range of techniques and projects. Full-colour step-by-step photographs appear throughout the book, plus explanatory illustrations, useful charts and a wealth of practical advice on creating the ideal interior.

DECORATING DECISIONS

The hardest part of any do-it-yourself project is deciding precisely what is wanted and planning how to achieve it. The decision may simply involve a choice of colour or pattern, or may be more complex, perhaps involving major changes to the style, layout, features and fittings of a room or rooms.

For example, it may seem likely that better use can be made of the interior space that is available. An easy way of doing this is to rearrange or change some of the furniture, whether it is freestanding or built-in – but a more radical approach may bring even more dramatic gains. Partitioning some rooms, linking others, even changing the use to which individual rooms have previously been put, can revolutionize the way a home works. This approach is particularly relevant as the occupants' needs alter over the years, since a house that worked well with young children will not suit a family with teenagers, and once the children have flown the nest their parents will want to use the house in a different way again.

On a smaller scale, even the way in which individual rooms are decorated and furnished can have a major effect on the way they look and feel. Many people find that achieving the style they want is often a process of evolution rather than revolution; few people can get everything right first time. The secret of success lies in understanding the basic rules of colour scheming and in learning how to make the best use of the wide range of materials and techniques available to the interior designer today.

Lastly, it also means taking a close look at what lighting contributes to the scheme. Few homes make use of the possibilities explored so imaginatively in many public buildings, yet some minor changes to lighting could bring a home alive. Some interior designers even dream of the day when they can create and change interior colour schemes with the flick of a switch. However, until that day the big decorating decisions are still the same as they always were; this chapter should render them somewhat easier to make.

Opposite: The art of successful decoration lies in marrying materials that protect and enhance the various surfaces around the home with a touch of decorative flair and originality that will give every room a style all its own and reflect the owner's personal taste and lifestyle.

MAKING AN ASSESSMENT

The best way to get an objective view of a home's interior condition is to imagine that it is up for sale and to view it in the role of a prospective purchaser. The aim of the exercise is not to give rise to a severe bout of depression, but to make it clear what exists in the home and what could be done to change or improve it.

Start at the front door, and step into the hallway. Is it bright and well lit, or gloomy and unwelcoming? A lighter colour scheme could make a narrow room appear more spacious, and better lighting would make it seem more inviting. Decorating the wall opposite the front door would make a long hall appear shorter, while changing the way the staircase is decorated could make it a less – or more – dominant feature. Is the staircase well lit, for safety's sake as well as for looks? Opening up the space beneath the stairs could get rid of what

Above: Choose an integrated decorating scheme for hallways, stairs and landing areas. Bring down the apparent ceiling height using a dado (chair) rail or decorative border.

Below: The living room has to be light and airy during the day, yet cosy and comfortable in the evening. The fireplace and a central table provide the main focal points here.

is typically an untidy gloryhole (storage room), taking up space without saving any. Lastly, are the wall and floor coverings practical? The hall floor is bound to be well trodden, and needs to be durable and easy to clean as well as looking attractive.

Now move into the main living room. This is always the most difficult room in the house to decorate and furnish successfully because of its dual purpose. It is used both for daily life and to entertain visitors. It must be fresh and lively by day, yet cosy and peaceful in the evening. One of the chief keys to success is flexible lighting that can be altered to suit the room's different uses, but the decorations and furnishings all have their part to play too.

Look at the colour scheme. How well does it blend in with the furnishings, the curtains and drapes, the floor covering? Are there any interesting features such as a fireplace, an alcove, an archway into another room, even an ornate cornice around the ceiling? Some might benefit from being highlighted, other less attractive ones would be better disguised.

Next, examine how the room works. Are traffic routes congested? Are the seating arrangements flexible? Are there surfaces where things can easily be put down? Does any storage or display provision look good and work well? Can everyone who is seated see the television? Does everyone want to? Assessing the room in this way reveals its successes and failures, and shows how to eliminate the latter.

Continue the guided tour with the dining room – or dining area, if it is part of a through room. This is often the least used room in the house, so its design tends to be neglected. Since it is usually used for just one purpose –

Left: Bedrooms are the most private of rooms, and their colour schemes and furnishings should reflect the personal whims of their occupants.

Below: The kitchen is the engine room of the house. It must be well-planned with plenty of work and storage space, and be pleasant to work in and easy to clean.

eating – it needs to be decorated in a way that avoids visual indigestion. Warm, welcoming colour schemes and flexible lighting work best in this location; strident patterns and harsh colours are to be avoided.

Now turn to the kitchen. Whatever type of room it is, the most important thing is that it should be hygienic, for obvious reasons. Are the various surfaces in the room easy to keep clean, and to redecorate when necessary? Are there dust and grease traps? Is the lighting over the hob (burners) and counter tops adequate? Is the floor covering a practical choice? Since the kitchen is often the hub of family life, it needs to be functional but adaptable, and also pleasant to be in so that the cook does not mind the time spent slaving over a hot stove.

Bathrooms have their own special requirements, mainly revolving around combining comfort with a degree of waterproofing, especially if there are young children in the family. Are the decorations and floor covering suitable? How do they complement the bathroom suite? What about the space available within the room? Could congestion be relieved by moving

things around? – or by moving them out altogether: having a shower instead of a bath could create lots of extra space. Could a second bathroom be created elsewhere in the house? Otherwise, putting washbasins in some of the bedrooms could take the pressure off the family bathroom during the morning rush hour.

Lastly, bedrooms. In most, the bed is the focal point of the room, so the way it is dressed will be the main influence on the room's appearance. The colour scheme also has its part to play in making the room look comfortable and relaxing; remember that the room's occupant will see it from two viewpoints – on entering, and from the bed – so take this into account when assessing it. What about the ceiling? In the one room where people actually spend some time staring at it, does it deserve something a little more adventurous than white paint? Is the floor covering warm to the touch of bare feet? In children's rooms, is it also capable of withstanding the occasional rough and tumble or a disaster with the finger paints? Lastly, is the lighting satisfactory? Most bedrooms need a combination of subdued general

lighting and brighter local task lighting for things such as reading in bed, putting on make-up or tackling school homework. Some changes may make the room work a great deal more satisfactorily.

Once the tour of the house is complete there should be a clear picture of its condition and how well it works; and some ideas as to how it might be improved. Above all, it will have been viewed as a whole, not just as a series of individual rooms. That is the first step towards creating an attractive, stylish and above all practical home.

Above: Bathrooms need tailoring to family needs. Here a double vanity unit provides valuable extra washing facilities for busy couples or growing families.

REORGANIZING SPACE

If a home does not function well, there are three choices. Two of these are thoroughly defeatist and may also be impractical: learn to live with it, or move to a more suitable house. The third is much more positive; alter it so that it gives the extra living space and the additional features needed.

The average home is basically a box, within which internal partitions create individual rooms, doors allow movement and windows let in light and air. Various services are included within the structure – heating, plumbing, wiring and so on. All these features can be altered, within reason, to make them work better.

When planning alterations, there are two considerations which should constantly be borne in mind. Are the changes feasible? And are they legal? It is essential to check with the local planning (zoning) and building control bodies to find out whether the work requires official approval.

Where to improve

Alterations to the use of space in the home are of two kinds. The first is to create new living space. The second is to alter the present layout of the interior and to change or improve the services. Here are some of the possibilities.

In the attic, unused space beneath a pitched roof could well become valuable extra living space. Remember, though, that providing access to the new rooms will mean losing some space on the floor below.

In the existing upstairs rooms, rearranging internal walls could create an extra bedroom or bathroom, while providing plumbing facilities in bedrooms could ease the pressure on the existing bathroom.

Above: Subdividing large rooms can help to create more effective use of space, by redefining traffic zones and providing more wall space for furniture.

Left: Bathing facilities are often over-stretched, especially in family homes. Finding the space for an extra shower cubicle can greatly relieve the traffic jams.

Right: Redesigning the kitchen provides the opportunity to rationalize both storage needs and work patterns. Modern fitted kitchens can cater for every individual requirement.

Downstairs, removing dividing walls to create large through rooms or partitioning large rooms to create two smaller ones, moving doorways to improve traffic flow, or altering the kitchen layout could all be considered. It might even be possible to turn an integral garage into extra living space.

Look at the possibility of changing the use to which individual rooms are

CONVERTING AN ATTIC

A full-scale conversion into one or more habitable rooms – that is, bedrooms and the like rather than just play or hobby space – is one of the biggest and most complex indoor home improvement projects. It involves altering the roof structure to make space for the rooms, strengthening the existing attic floor, providing access from the floor below, installing roof or dormer windows and extending existing services into the new rooms. Professional advice is needed here, and it is advisable to hand over the main structural alterations to a builder or specialist conversion firm. That still leaves plenty of scope for do-it-yourself finishing and fitting of the new rooms.

In many older homes, the space beneath a pitched (sloping) roof can be used to provide valuable extra living space, often with spectacular results.

put, especially if the family is increasing or decreasing in size. Reorganization can bring dramatic improvements to the way the house works.

Creating a through room
Creating a through room means removing an existing dividing wall, and may also require the repositioning of existing doorways and the formation of new windows. If the existing wall is loadbearing, a steel beam will have to be installed to carry the load, and lintels will also be needed over new windows and over new doors in other loadbearing walls. It may be necessary to reroute existing plumbing and electrical services that cross the wall that will be removed. Once the new opening has been formed, there will be extensive replastering to be done, and the floors in the two rooms will have to be linked smoothly. The original colour schemes of the two rooms will also probably be different, which may entail complete redecoration.

Partitioning an existing room
Subdividing an existing room into two smaller ones means building a new wall, possibly adding a door or window to one of the new rooms, and perhaps altering or extending existing plumbing, heating and electrical services to serve the two separate rooms.

The new dividing wall will generally be built as a timber-framed partition wall faced with plasterboard (gypsum board), but a solid blockwork wall could be built on suitable foundations, which may well need to be inserted.

Creating a new door opening
If the new opening is to be made in a loadbearing wall, a lintel must be used to bridge the opening. However, if the wall is a non-loadbearing partition, simple alterations to the wall framing are all that will be needed. The job will also involve some replastering work, making alterations to skirtings (baseboards) and floor surfaces, the fitting of architraves (trims) around the opening, and possibly alterations to existing plumbing, heating and electrical services if pipes or cables cross the area where the door will be installed.

Altering the kitchen layout
The amount of work depends on how extensive the rearrangement will be. At the very least there will be new base and wall units (cabinets) and counter tops, and these will probably involve some work on wall and floor surfaces. If repositioning sinks, cookers (stoves), dishwashers and the like, there will have to be alterations to plumbing and electrical services.

USING COLOUR, PATTERN AND TEXTURE

After redesigning the house layout and reorganizing each room, the next task is to start planning the colour schemes. To do this successfully, it helps to understand the basics of colour theory, and how to use pattern and texture to good effect.

When putting a colour scheme together, a device called the *colour wheel* can be used to help plan the various decorative effects. All colours are made by mixing together varying proportions of the three *primary* colours – red, yellow and blue. Mixing them in pairs creates three new *secondary* colours, with red and yellow making orange, yellow and blue making green, and blue and red making violet. Imagine these six colours making up segments of a circle in the order red, orange, yellow, green, blue and violet. Mix adjacent pairs together again, and you create six *tertiary* colours – red/orange, orange/yellow, yellow/green, green/blue, blue/violet and violet/red. Adding these to the circle gives the basic colour wheel of twelve segments.

There is one more ingredient to add to these colours: colour intensity or tone. By adding different amounts of white or black, you can produce lighter or darker shades of the original colours in almost infinite variety. And you can also, of course, use white, black and varying shades of grey as colours in their own right.

On the wheel, the twelve colours split into two groups. The colours from violet/red round to yellow are known as *advancing* colours because they appear to make wall and ceiling surfaces look nearer to the viewer than they really are. They make a room seem warm and welcoming, but also smaller. The remaining colours are known as *receding* colours because they have the opposite

THE COLOUR WHEEL

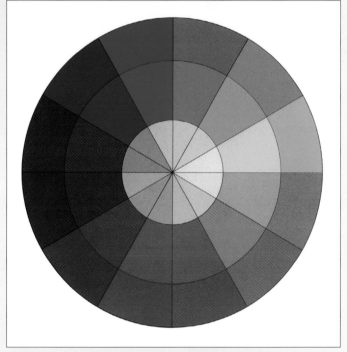

An understanding of colour and colour mixing will be invaluable when choosing a new colour scheme. The colour wheel is divided into 12 segments, and the central ring shows the primary, secondary and tertiary colours described in the text. The outer ring shows darker tones of these colours and the inner one lighter ones.

Left: Blues, greys and plenty of white space create a cool, airy colour scheme that is the perfect complement for wooden fixtures and furnishings in a light shade of pine.

Left: Blues and greens are naturally cool, receding colours, ideal for well-lit south-facing rooms, but can be warmed by splashes of contrast in orange and yellow.

Above: Neutral tones – beiges, creams and browns – create a colour scheme that is restful on the eye and can be teemed with almost any accessory shades.

visual effect, making a room look cool, and also larger than in reality. Which group is chosen as the basis for a colour scheme depends on the overall effect that is wanted in that particular room.

The colour wheel also helps to create colour *harmony* or *contrast*. Colours next to or near each other are said to be in colour harmony, giving a restful effect. However, too much colour harmony can become visually rather dull; it needs livening up with some elements of colour contrast, which come from using colours at opposite sides of the wheel. Colours exactly opposite each other, such as red and green, are called *complementary*. The ideal colour scheme is usually considered to be a basically harmonious one, with contrast added by the judicious use of contrasting or complementary colours for some elements of the design. Soft furnishing, such as scatter cushions or blinds and shades, chosen in a fabric to contrast with the overall colour scheme can add just the right amount of contrast to brighten up a room.

Below: Nothing succeeds in creating a feeling of cosiness as well as the red/pink section of the colour wheel. Surface texture plays its part too, as does warm, natural wood fittings.

USING COLOUR, PATTERN AND TEXTURE *(continued)*

Left: Bold splashes of colour can add interest and definition to a colour scheme that is basically neutral.

Below: Wall coverings with a vertical pattern element can help to make rooms appear taller, but work well only when the walls are perfectly square.

Colour can also play tricks on the eye, which can be used to good effect in colour scheming. For example, painting a high ceiling in a dark colour makes it appear lower. The same effect applies on walls, where using dark colour on opposite walls makes a wide room seem narrower; conversely, using it on the end wall of a long, thin room and lighter colours on the side walls helps to make the room seem wider to the eye.

Using pattern

Pattern on walls, ceilings and floors adds visual interest to a colour scheme, either in harmony with the overall effect or to provide contrast – for example, by having a patterned wall covering on one wall, and the rest painted. Pattern as well as colour can cheat the eye and alter the apparent dimensions of a room. Wall coverings with a distinct horizontal pattern make walls seem wider and ceilings lower; strong vertical designs such as stripes have the opposite effect. The same applies to pattern in floor coverings, which can make a room look wider or narrower depending on which way the pattern element runs.

Pattern size has its own contribution to make. Wall and floor coverings with large pattern motifs make the surface they are on seem to advance and so make the room appear smaller, while tiny motifs have the opposite effect of making the surface appear to recede from the eye. Choosing patterned fabrics for cushions, curtains and drapes or bed linen is an ideal way of enlivening a decor with plain walls and woodwork.

Above: Small, random patterns are a better choice than larger motifs for small rooms, and are ideal for decorating areas where perfect pattern matching can be difficult.

Left: Luxurious fabrics used for curtains, cushions and upholstery are often the ideal medium for adding patterned elements to a decor.

Using texture

Surface texture – in other words, a surface that is not completely smooth – helps to add variety and visual interest to your colour schemes. Wall coverings with a textured or embossed surface generally have a comparatively low relief which helps to soften the decorative effect of the material, while texture paints can be used to create effects that have quite a high relief and consequently look particularly striking when lit from the side. Textured finishes also have another benefit, of helping to disguise slightly irregular wall and ceiling surfaces.

Right: Sometimes richly textured upholstery and floor coverings benefit from the simplest of settings. Here textured walls and painted floorboards in pure white are the perfect backdrop.

LIGHTING BASICS

Good lighting can play an important role in bringing a home to life, as well as making it easier for the occupants to work and engage in leisure activities. Few homes take advantage of the design possibilities that good lighting can offer, preferring to rely on the traditional central pendant light in each room and the occasional table or standard (standing) lamp.

The following pages show some of the many versatile and attractive lighting effects that can be achieved in different rooms. Before embarking on a radical redesign of a lighting scheme it is important to understand some of the basics of lighting design.

Light is provided by lamps and tubes of various types and wattages. *Wattage* is a measurement of the amount of electricity the lamp consumes. The amount of light each emits is measured in units called *lumens*. Conventional

Below: Where lamps are visible, it is best to use types such as candles and globes that look attractive whether lit or unlit.

HOW LAMPS EMIT LIGHT

Fluorescent tubes (**1**) and GLS (general lighting service) lamps (**2**) emit light in all directions. Silvered reflectors emit it either forwards (**3, 4, 5**) or backwards (**6**).

tungsten-filament lamps – that is, ordinary lightbulbs – are much less efficient at producing light than are fluorescent tubes. For example, a 40-watt lamp emits about 400 lumens, or 10 lumens per watt of power used, while a 40-watt tube emits almost 2000 lumens, or 50 lumens per watt.

The amount of light that is needed depends on the surface area being lit. As a general guide something in the region of 200 lumens per sq m (20 lumens per sq ft) is needed in work areas such as kitchens, half that figure in other living rooms, bathrooms and in access areas such as halls, landings and stairs, and a quarter of the amount – 50 lumens per sq m (5 lumens per sq ft) in bedrooms.

Above: Individual spotlights on ceiling- or wall-mounted track provide the maximum flexibility when highlighting particular room features.

There are other factors to take into consideration when working out how much light is needed, such as the colour and reflectivity of the surfaces being lit and whether lighting is direct or indirect, but they are somewhat complex for the lay person to work with. As a rough guide for general background lighting, using filament lighting emitting around 10 lumens per watt, aim to provide about 20 watts per sq m (2 watts per sq ft) of floor area. As an example, a living room measuring 6 × 4 m (20 × 13 ft) would need 6 × 4 × 20 = 480 watts of lighting. For fluorescent tubes giving 50 lumens per watt, you need 4 watts per sq m (0.4 watts per sq ft) – that is, just under 100 watts of lighting for the same room. Regard any additional local task lighting in the room, for reading or studying perhaps, as supplementary to this basic figure.

Left: Globe lamps have an opaque spherical envelope that is perfect for use with pendant fittings, and look good whether the light is on or off.

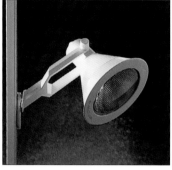

Above: Downlighters (**left**) and PAR reflectors (**right**) can cast a narrow spotlight beam or create a border floodlit effect, according to the type of lamp fitted.

HOW LIGHT FITTINGS EMIT LIGHT

The type of light fitting or lampshade used affects the way light is distributed. Shown here are a pendant lampshade (**1**), a ceiling-mounted diffuser (**2**), wall lights with diffusers (**3**), spotlights on ceiling-mounted track (**4**), a downlighter (**5**), a recessed eyeball (**6**), a wallwasher (**7**) and an uplighter (**8**).

Above: Wall-mounted uplighters are used to wash ceilings with light. When fitted with a crown-silvered lamp, the light source is invisible even with the lamp at eye level.

LIGHTING FOR LIVING AND DINING ROOMS

The key to success with any lighting scheme is to ensure that it meets two criteria: it must give light where it is needed; and the effect it creates should enhance the room's appearance by creating a balanced mixture of light and shadow. The type of light fittings chosen has a major part to play, and so does the positioning of the fittings. The illustration shows how the type and positioning of ceiling lights can create different lighting effects on room walls.

The first basic guideline to observe is to ensure that naked lamps or tubes cannot be seen, by the judicious choice of shades and diffusers. The second is always to provide an acceptable level of background lighting throughout the room, even when additional local lighting is employed, to avoid creating pools of hard, dark shadow. The third is to use lighting to highlight individual features of the room – an attractive alcove, for example, lit by a spotlight, or a run of curtains (drapes) illuminated by perimeter lighting.

In addition, many rooms in the house will probably need local task lighting, for reading, writing, sewing or other work. The kitchen in particular has its own special lighting requirements. Some task lighting requirements can be satisfied by the use of portable plug-in lamps, while others may need more permanent arrangements.

Living rooms are among the most difficult areas to light successfully, because of the many different uses to which the room is put. The aim should be to provide background lighting that can be bright or dim according to the

Above: A rise-and-fall fitting provides glare-free light over the dining table, while a freestanding uplighter casts a gentle glow across the ceiling.

Right: Recessed eyeball spotlights allow light to be focussed closely on individual features or objects in a room, and can be adjusted as required.

Above: For lighting with minimal glare, team an opaque central fitting with strip lights behind pelmets (valances) to light up a cornice (crown molding) and the ceiling surface above.

Opposite: Pastel-shaded lamps in opaque lampshades help to create soft background lighting effects that complement the room's colour scheme.

mood of the moment, and then to add separately controllable feature lighting to highlight the room's focal points, and local task lighting where required. The accent is on flexibility. Choosing fittings in keeping with the style of the room will help to ensure that its lighting looks good by day or by night.

Dining rooms have slightly different needs. The main requirement is a table that is well lit without glare, which you can satisfy with a rise-and-fall fitting or carefully targeted downlighters. The background lighting should be subdued, preferably under dimmer control – note that fluorescent lights cannot be easily dimmed. Additional lighting from wall lights or wallwashers can be used to illuminate the serving and carving area, and uplighters for dramatic effect.

WASHING WALLS WITH LIGHT

A row of wallwashers of the same wattage create a perfect wash (**1**); decreasing wattages along the row give a graded wash (**2**). A row of downlighters can create a scalloped effect (**3**); a single downlighter casts a parabola (**4**).

LIGHTING FOR KITCHENS AND BATHROOMS

Below: Kitchens are difficult to light because most tasks take place round the perimeter of the room. Lights above counter tops are the perfect solution.

Kitchens pose special lighting problems mainly owing to the wide use of the fitted kitchen. In the old days most food preparation was done on a central table, so a central light was generally adequate. Now almost every task is carried out close to the perimeter of the room, and a central light – still the standard fitting in many homes – is now useless, condemning the cook to working in his or her own shadow.

What a modern kitchen needs is lighting tailored to provide good illumination at each of the main work stations – the cooker (stove), the sink and the food preparation area. There should also be a reasonable level of general background lighting, plus lighting to illuminate the insides of cupboards (closets). These requirements can only be achieved by separate, flexible and independently controllable light sources.

If the cooker has an extractor hood over it, one containing a downlighter will illuminate the hob (burners) satisfactorily. Otherwise the aim should be to provide ceiling-mounted lights positioned so that they shine directly on the hob without casting a shadow. The same is needed over the sink. Ideally each of these lights or sets of lights should have its own switch so that it can be switched on and off as required. For counter tops below wall storage units, lighting is best provided by striplights fixed beneath the wall units and shielded by baffles to prevent glare. Walk-in cupboards and open display units can be lit by recessed downlighters, and base units can be lit by small interior lights with automatic switches worked by opening the doors. If the kitchen is also used for eating, provide a rise-and-fall fitting or recessed downlighters over the kitchen table so

that the rest of the kitchen lighting can be turned off – not least to hide the cooking debris during the meal.

Bathrooms are much less demanding. The basic requirement is for a modest level of background lighting, provided by a close-mounted central light or some recessed fittings. If the washbasin area is used for shaving or applying

make-up, add a wall strip (fluorescent) light over the basin to provide good, glare-free illumination there. Do not install a fluorescent light if it is to be used for applying make-up. Even the best types give a slightly inaccurate rendering of some colours. There may also be a need for a splashproof recessed light fitting in a shower cubicle.

Above: Track lighting is a versatile solution for kitchens and utility rooms, since individual spots can be adjusted to cast light where it is most wanted.

Above: In bathrooms, enclosed fittings are a must for safety reasons. A central fitting with an opaque diffuser will cast a soft overall light.

Left: Recessed downlighters can be used in bathrooms to provide some additional illumination above areas such as vanity units.

LIGHTING IN BEDROOMS

Bedroom lighting requires a combination of restful background lighting and easily controllable local lighting to cover separate activities such as dressing and undressing, applying make-up, reading in bed, or perhaps watching television. Remember that every fitting must look as good from the viewpoint of the bed as from elsewhere in the room.

Background lighting can be provided by wall lights, by table lamps on bedside tables, by recessed downlighters or, very appropriately for bedrooms, with the wall- or ceiling-mounted fittings known as uplighters, which throw light onto the ceiling and completely conceal the lamp when viewed from below. The general light level can be lower than for living rooms, as long as the task lighting does its job. Bright,

glare-free lighting is needed at a dressing table, and good light from above to check clothes. Fluorescent lighting should not be used here, because it falsifies certain colours, so choose ordinary lightbulbs.

Bedside reading lights should be directional so that they illuminate the page adequately but do not disturb a sleeping partner. Lastly, make full use of two-way switching so that lights can be turned on and off without having to get out of bed. Again, choose light fittings to complement the room's decor and colour scheme.

Children's rooms, especially nurseries, have slightly different requirements. Good task lighting is essential for jobs such as changing or dressing a baby, and young children will want a higher overall lighting level

than in an adult's room when playing. They may also need a low-wattage night light for comfort and safety. Finally, older children will want portable task lighting for activities such as hobbies and homework.

The landing and stairwell should not be forgotten. This is one area of the home where good bright lighting is essential; safety is more important than mood here, ensuring that all parts of the staircase are clearly lit without glare. For the best effect, fittings should be positioned so that treads are lit but risers are in shadow. Make sure that any suspended fittings do not impede passage up and down the staircase, and check that recessed fittings are readily accessible – it is irritating to have to get a ladder out to reach a high-level fitting whenever a lamp fails.

Above: Recessed downlighters are the ideal light source for children's rooms, providing good illumination of play and storage areas yet remaining safely out of harm's way.

Left: An opaque shade on a bedside light prevents glare while providing gentle background uplighting and enough downlighting for bedtime reading.

Right: In bedrooms, light fittings need careful selection because they must look as attractive from the bed as from elsewhere in the room. Globe lamps look good and are free from glare.

Below: In nurseries, low-energy fluorescent lamps offer the ideal combination of long life and safety, since the lamp envelope is cool to the touch.

Above: Halls and stairwells need good illumination for safety reasons. Here recessed downlighters illuminate every tread of the staircase and highlight the hall's features too.

Above: A wall-mounted downlighter can also be used to safely light a staircase, casting the risers into shadow and so making the treads more clearly visible.

LIGHTING FOR DISPLAY AND SECURITY

Most of the lighting schemes mentioned so far have concentrated on illuminating individual rooms and providing good task lighting for the various activities carried out in them. However, lighting can also be used as a means of decorating rooms and highlighting their best features.

Spotlights offer great flexibility here. They are available as single, double and triple spot units for wall or ceiling mounting, as individual spotlights designed to fit on lighting track, or as recessed 'eyeball' ceiling fittings. The beam direction can be adjusted to 'wash' walls, curtains (drapes) or ceilings with light, which may be coloured instead of white; or to illuminate an individual area of the room such as a fireplace, an arch, an alcove, a display unit (cabinet) or some other feature.

Small spotlights, especially the recessed eyeball types, can be used to illuminate individual pictures or picture groups on your walls. Alternatively, a traditional picture light – a small strip light in a wall-mounted holder – may be set above or below the picture.

Shelves or closed cabinets displaying china, glass or other *objets d' art* can be lit in several ways. Spotlighting is one, but this can look harsh. What often works better is either backlighting via small tungsten filament strip lights fitted beneath the shelves or, where glass shelves are used, a lamp behind a frosted glass panel at the top or bottom of the unit.

That last area of lighting that is well worth considering is indoor security lighting. It is well known that intruders are deterred by good lighting outside the house; this also applies indoors, for several reasons. The first is that if a would-be intruder sees an indoor light,

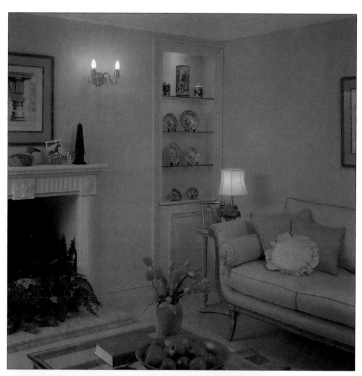

he can never be sure whether the house is occupied or not, especially if the curtains are drawn. Even if the owners are out, he will be less keen to break in and risk being seen from outside.

There are several types of programmable controls which can be used to switch both fixed lighting and plug-in lights on, either at preset times or at sunset. Some can then mimic human behaviour by turning lights on and off at random during the night, and will switch off at dawn. Others turn lights on – and can also trigger a burglar alarm – if they detect the body heat of an intruder, much like the sensors used out of doors. All give extra protection, especially if combined with electrically controlled curtain closers.

Above: Pictures can be brought to life if highlighted by an individual spotlight or a linear picture light.

Opposite: Low-voltage tungsten halogen lighting sheds a crisp white light that is perfect for highlighting a collection of ornamental glass.

Above: Coloured lamps can help to accentuate a room's colour scheme, while concealed lighting in display alcoves makes the most of china and other treasures.

Left: Use a combination of small clip-on spotlights and freestanding fittings to cast individual pools of light on decorative objects within an alcove.

PLANNING THE WORK

Once it is clear exactly what work is to be carried out in the home, it is essential to plan the job properly so as to do things in a sensible order. This will not only ensure that the work proceeds smoothly, with the minimum of disruption to family life; it will also help in estimating accurately the quantities of materials needed for each phase of the job, and to check that all the necessary tools and materials are to hand, including hired equipment.

Where to start depends on how extensive the work is. Begin with any major internal alterations such as building partition walls; creating through rooms; relocating rooms; adding or blocking off windows and doorways; removing, blocking or opening up chimney breasts; and lowering ceilings. Then carry out any alterations that are needed to the services – for example electric wiring, plumbing or heating pipework – whether this is to improve them generally or to cope with the alterations. If merely repainting or covering a wall, remove existing furniture, fixtures and fittings in order to strip out any materials that are to be replaced, or to prepare existing surfaces. At this stage, there is an opportunity to tackle any general repairs that may be required to make good the wall, floor, ceiling and woodwork surfaces, before starting work on the new scheme.

Finally, complete the work in each room by replacing the fixtures and fittings, followed by bringing in existing or replacement furniture and adding the soft furnishings.

STEP-BY-STEP CHECKLIST

Use this checklist to help in organizing
each numbered stage of the work and to
draw up a record of the tools, equipment
and materials required.

Task	Materials	Tools/equipment
1 Remove furniture from affected room(s)		
2 Remove fixtures and fittings: go to 7 if not carrying out major work		
3 Carry out structural alterations		
4 Relocate room contents		
5 Alter/extend/improve services		
6 Replace features (doors, mouldings/trims etc.) being altered		
7 Remove old wall and floor covering materials being replaced		
8 Make good any damaged surfaces		
9 Wash or rub down painted wall/ceiling surfaces		
10 Wash or rub down painted woodwork		
11 Clean floors, level surface if uneven		
12 Paint or paper ceilings		
13 Paint or cover walls		
14 Paint woodwork		
15 Fix wall tiles/cladding (panelling)		
16 Add decorative mouldings, borders etc.		
17 Replace fixtures and fittings (light switches shelf brackets, curtain (drapery) track, built-in furniture etc.)		
18 Lay new floor coverings		
19 Reposition furniture		
20 Add soft furnishings (curtains/drapes, blinds/shades, cushions etc.)		

PAINTING

Painting walls, woodwork and other surfaces is, so all the surveys reveal, by far the most popular do-it-yourself job. Modern paints and improvements in the design and manufacture of decorating tools have certainly made the task less arduous than it was in the days of traditional oil-bound paints and distemper, and have also made it easier for the amateur decorator to get professional-looking results.

One major shift in paint technology is the trend away from using solvent-based varnishes and paints for wood, towards water-based products which do not give off harmful vapours as they dry. Water-based finishes are not as durable as solvent-based ones, but are no longer as far behind them in performance terms as they once were, and they have other advantages such as faster drying times, virtually no smell and easier cleaning of brushes, rollers and pads. It is therefore likely that their use in the home will become much more widespread.

No amount of clever technology can eliminate the need for proper preparation of the surfaces to be decorated, even though this part of the job is far less enjoyable and often more time-consuming than the actual painting. In many cases it will involve little other than washing the surface down, but sometimes more thorough preparation will be called for.

This chapter describes the various types of paint, varnish and stain on the market; which to use where; how to prepare surfaces for redecoration; how to apply the new finish – especially to the more awkward surfaces such as windows and panelled doors – and how to create a range of special paint effects that can be a dramatic and inexpensive alternative to wall coverings.

Opposite: Paint offers a huge palette of colours, and complementary and contrasting shades can create the subtlest and most restful of colour schemes. It is the easiest finish to change too when a room needs a new look.

TYPES OF PAINT, VARNISH AND STAIN

Paint works by forming a film on the surface to which it is applied. This film has to do three things: it must hide the surface underneath; it must protect it; and it must stay put. All paint has three main ingredients: pigment, binder and carrier. The *pigment* gives the film its colour and hiding power. The *binder* binds the pigment particles together into a continuous film as the paint dries, and also bonds the film to the surface beneath. In traditional paint this was a natural material such as linseed oil in oil paints, or glue size in distemper; but modern paints use synthetic resins such as alkyd, acrylic, vinyl and polyurethane. The third ingredient, the *carrier*, makes the paint flow smoothly as it is applied, and evaporates as the paint dries.

The ratio of pigment to binder in a paint affects the finish it has when it dries; the higher the pigment content, the duller the finish. By adjusting this ratio, paint manufacturers can produce paints that dry to a flat *matt* finish; to a silky sheen, *eggshell*; or to a high *gloss*. The choice depends on personal preference, tempered by the condition of the surface: high-gloss finishes highlight any imperfections, while matt finishes tend to disguise them.

Paint types

The paint types used in the home have different carriers. Water-based paint has the pigment and binder suspended in water as tiny droplets. It is an emulsion, like milk, and is usually called *emulsion* paint. (In the USA it is

Above: The yellow water-based paint chosen for the walls of this kitchen creates a basically warm colour scheme that is off-set by the gloss paint in cool colours selected for the woodwork. Solvent-based (oil) paint is ideal for surfaces which need washing down regularly.

Left: There is nothing like a hint of strong contrast to bring a neutral colour scheme to life, as the bright red bedposts and picture rail do so dramatically here. Paints specially formulated for steamy locations should be used in en-suite bathrooms.

Right: Blues and greys are cool, fresh colours that particularly suit a well-lit children's room. The brightly painted ladder provides the perfect contrast. Painted surfaces need to be able to withstand some rough treatment in these locations.

Paint systems

A single coat of paint is too thin to form a durable paint film. To provide adequate cover and performance there must be a paint system consisting of several coats. What these are depends on the type of paint used, and on the surface being painted.

The first coat is a *sealer*, which is used where necessary to seal in things such as the natural resin in wood, or to prevent the paint from soaking into a porous surface.

The second is a *primer*, which provides a good key for the paint film to stick to. On metal surfaces, this also stops the metal corroding or oxidizing. A primer can also act as a sealer.

The third is the *undercoat*, which builds up the film to form a flexible,

often called *latex* paint.) As the water evaporates the droplets coalesce to form the paint film. Solvent-based *alkyd* paints have pigment and binder dissolved in a petroleum-based solvent, and take longer to dry than water-based paints. (In the USA these are known as *oil* or *oil-base* paints, though the term 'alkyd' is used for some primers of this kind.) These paints give off a characteristic 'painty' smell as they dry, which many people find unpleasant and to which some are actually allergic. Because of growing awareness of the health risks of inhaling some solvents, the use of these paints is declining in popularity and is already legally restricted in some countries.

Paint also contains a range of other additives to improve its performance. The most notable is one that makes the paint *thixotropic* or non-drip, allowing more paint to be loaded onto the brush and a thicker paint film to be applied; one coat is often sufficient.

Above: A palette of yellow shades adds up to an irresistibly welcoming colour scheme for a baby's nursery.

Left: Paint is not only for walls, ceilings and woodwork; it can also help to enhance the crisp lines of ornamental plasterwork.

TYPES OF PAINT, VARNISH AND STAIN *(continued)*

Below: Plain painted walls can be given a personal touch with hand-painted embellishments. Decorators with unsteady hands can use stencils instead.

Above: Sponging a second colour over a complementary base coat creates a soft broken-colour effect.

Above: Rag-rolling is another broken-colour effect that can look especially attractive when applied in stripes over the base colour.

non-absorbent base of uniform colour close to that of the fourth and final layer, the *top coat*, which gives the actual finish and colour.

On walls, for which water-based paint is generally used, the system consists simply of two or three coats of the same paint unless there is a need for a sealer or primer to cure a fault in the surface such as dustiness, high alkalinity or excessive porosity. The first coat is a *mist* coat of thinned paint. A primer is also used if walls are being painted with solvent-based paints.

On woodwork, the first step is to apply a liquid called *knotting* (shellac) to any knots to prevent resin from bleeding through the paint film. Then comes a wood primer, which may be water-based or solvent-based, followed by an undercoat and then the top coat. To speed up the painting process, paint manufacturers have now perfected combined primer/undercoats, and have also introduced so-called *self-undercoating* gloss paint which just needs a primer.

On metal, a primer is generally needed. A zinc phosphate primer is used for iron or steel, and there are special primers for aluminium. This is then followed by an undercoat and top coat, as for wood. Copper, brass and lead can be painted directly without the need for a primer so long as they are brought to a bright finish first and are thoroughly degreased with white spirit (paint thinner).

Varnishes and wood stains

Varnish is basically paint without the pigment. Most contain polyurethane resins and are solvent-based (like oil paint), although water-based acrylic varnishes are becoming more popular for health and environmental reasons,

CLEANING PAINTING EQUIPMENT

Paint is thinned or diluted if necessary with water or white spirit (paint thinner) according to the paint type. Wash tools and equipment in soapy water if using a water-based paint, and with white spirit or a proprietary brush cleaner for solvent-based (oil) paint. Soak hardened paint in paint remover overnight, then wash out the softened paint with hot soapy water.

Above: Coloured varnishes help to enhance the colour of the wood grain without obliterating it completely, as paint does.

Above: Varnish is a hardwearing alternative to paint on wood with an attractive grain pattern, and the surface shows marks less readily than paint too.

just as solvent-based paints are losing ground to water-based types. Varnishes are available with a satin/silk or a high-gloss finish, either clear or with the addition of small amounts of colour. These coloured varnishes are intended to enhance the appearance of the wood, or to give it some extra colour without obliterating the wood grain, as paint would do.

Varnish is its own primer and undercoat, although it is best to thin the first coat with about 10 per cent white spirit (paint thinner) for solvent-based types, or water for acrylic types, and to apply it with a lint-free cloth rather than a brush so that it can be rubbed well into the wood grain. When this first coat has dried, it is *keyed* or roughened by rubbing very lightly with fine abrasive paper (sandpaper), dusted off, and a second, full-strength coat brushed on. For surfaces likely to get a lot of wear, it is advisable to key the second coat as before and apply an additional coat.

Wood stains, unlike paint and varnish, are designed to soak into the wood. They may subsequently be sealed

with clear varnish to improve the finish and make the surface more durable. They are available in water-based or solvent-based types in a wide range of colours and wood shades; different colours of the same type can be blended to obtain intermediate shades, and the stain can be thinned with water or white spirit as appropriate to give a paler effect.

Stains are often applied with a brush or a paint pad, but it is often quicker and easier to get even coverage by putting them on with a clean lint-free cloth. Quick work is needed to blend wet edges together, and to avoid overlaps which will leave darker patches as the stain dries. A water-based stain will raise fibres on the surface of the wood, which will spoil the evenness of the colour. The solution is to sand the surface perfectly smooth first and then dampen it with a wet cloth. This will raise the surface fibres. When the wood is dry these fibres are sanded off with extra-fine abrasive paper, ready to receive the application of stain.

Above: Varnish can be used to enhance the natural beauty of wood throughout the home, from floors and fire surrounds to storage units and other items of furniture.

PAINTING TOOLS AND EQUIPMENT

Two groups of tools are needed, one for preparing the surface and one for actually putting the paint on. For a masonry wall, the minimum preparation is to wash down any previously painted surface. This calls for a bucket, sponges and cloths, strong household detergent or sugar soap (all-purpose cleaner), and rubber gloves to protect the hands.

If the washed-down surface has a high-gloss finish, or feels rough to the touch, use fine abrasive paper (sandpaper) and a sanding block to smooth it down. Wet-and-dry (silicon carbide) paper, used wet, is best for sanding down existing paintwork; rinse off the resulting fine slurry of paint with water afterwards. Use ordinary abrasive paper for bare wood.

Defects in the surface need filling. Use a traditional cellulose filler (spackle) for small cracks, chips and other surface blemishes, and an expanding filler foam which can be shaped and sanded when hard for larger defects. To apply filler paste use a filling knife (putty knife).

To strip existing paintwork, use either a heat gun – easier to control and much safer to use than a blowtorch – or a chemical paint remover, plus scrapers of various shapes to remove the softened paint. For removing wall coverings in order to apply a painted wall or ceiling finish, a steam wallpaper stripper will be invaluable. The small all-in-one strippers which resemble a large steam iron are the easiest type to use.

Painting tools

The paintbrush is still the favourite tool for applying paint to walls, ceilings, woodwork and metalwork around the house. Most are made with natural bristle, held in a metal ferrule which is attached to a wooden or plastic handle, but there are also brushes with synthetic fibre bristles which are sometimes recommended for applying water-based (latex) paints.

Brushes come in widths from 12 mm ($^1/_2$ in) up to 150 mm (6 in). The smallest sizes are used for fiddly jobs such as painting glazing bars (muntins), while the widest are ideal for flat uninterrupted wall and ceiling surfaces. However, a wide brush can be tiring to use, especially with solvent-based (oil) paints. There are also long-handled

PREPARATION EQUIPMENT

The following tools and equipment are the general items needed to prepare for repainting: steam wallpaper stripper (**1**), liquid paint remover (**2**), paste paint remover (**3**), cellulose filler (spackle) (**4**), expanding filler foam (**5**), rubber gloves (**6**), bucket (**7**), sugar soap (all-purpose cleaner) (**8**), sponge (**9**), cloth (**10**), spray gun (**11**), abrasive paper (sandpaper) (**12**), sanding block (**13**), shavehooks (triangular scrapers) (**14**), scrapers (**15**), heat gun and attachments (a directional nozzle and two integral scrapers) (**16**).

brushes with angled heads for painting behind radiators, and narrow brushes called *cutting-in* (sash) brushes, which have the bristle tips cut off at an angle for painting into internal angles. For the best results, buy good-quality brushes and look after them, rather than buy cheap ones and throw them away after finishing the job.

Paint rollers are used mainly for painting walls and ceilings with water-based paints, although they can be used with solvent-based types too. They consist of a metal roller cage mounted on a handle, plus a hollow sleeve that fits onto the cage and actually applies the paint. Some can be fitted with an extension pole, which is useful if there are high ceilings or stairwells to paint. Most rollers are 180 mm (7 in) wide;

larger sizes are available, but can be harder to 'drive'. There are also slim mini-rollers for painting awkward-to-reach areas such as walls behind radiators. For any type, a roller tray is used to load paint onto the sleeve. Solid water-based paint is sold in its own tray.

The sleeves are waterproof tubes with a layer of foam plastic or cloth stuck to the outside. The second type may be made from natural or synthetic fibre, and have a short, medium or long pile. Choose the pile length to match the surface being painted: short for flat surfaces, medium for those with a slight texture and long for heavily embossed or sculpted surfaces.

Paint pads are squares or rectangles of short-pile cloth stuck to a foam backing

and mounted on a plastic or metal handle. The pad is dipped in a shallow container, or loaded from a special paint container with a roller feed, and then drawn across the surface. Pads come in a range of sizes.

Paint and varnish are also sold in *aerosol* form. This is ideal for small areas or fiddly materials such as wickerwork, but too expensive to use on large areas.

Lastly, do not forget the decorating sundries. A *paint kettle* is needed for decanting the paint and straining out any foreign bodies. Hand-held *paint masks* or *masking tape* are invaluable aids to getting straight edges and keeping paint off adjacent surfaces. Above all, remember to provide *dust sheets* (drop cloths), which perform better than plastic sheets.

PAINTING EQUIPMENT

This selection of equipment includes: brushes in various sizes (**1**), aerosol paint (**2**), long-handled brush for use behind radiators (**3**), hand-held skirting (baseboard) masks (**4**), slimline mini-roller (**5**), roller extension pole (**6**), a full-sized roller with short-pile sleeve and roller tray (**7**), dust sheet (drop cloth) (**8**), white spirit (paint thinner) (**9**), long pile and textured roller sleeves (**10**), paint shield (**11**), masking tape (**12**), paint kettle (**13**), paint pads in various sizes and shapes (**14**), paint-loading containers for paint pads (**15**).

PREPARING SURFACES FOR PAINTING

Modern paints have excellent adhesion and covering power, but to get the best performance from them they must be given a good start by preparing the surface thoroughly.

Wash surfaces, which have previously been painted, using a solution of strong household detergent or sugar soap (all-purpose cleaner). Rinse them very thoroughly with clean water, and allow them to dry completely before starting repainting.

Remove areas of flaking paint with a scraper or filling knife (putty knife), and then either touch in the bare area with more paint or fill it flush with the surrounding paint film by using fine filler (spackle). Sand this smooth when it has hardened.

If the surface shows signs of mildew growth due to persistent condensation, wipe it over with household bleach, or refrigerator cleaner containing a fungicide, to kill off the spores. Wash

down the surface with detergent and rinse thoroughly.

If knots are showing through on painted woodwork, sand the paint film back to bare wood and apply knotting (shellac) to the knot, then prime and undercoat to bring the new paint film level with the surrounding paintwork. Sand between coats. Resinous knots may produce stains which can only be prevented by drying the knot out with a blowtorch.

PREPARING PAINTED WOODWORK

1 Use fine-grade abrasive paper (sandpaper) wrapped around a sanding block to remove 'nibs' from the paint surface and to key the paint film ready for repainting.

2 Wash the surface down with detergent or sugar soap (all-purpose cleaner) to remove dirt, grease, finger marks and the dust from sanding it. Rinse with clean water, ensuring that no detergent residue is left as this will inhibit the new paint film.

3 Use a proprietary tack rag or a clean cloth moistened with white spirit (paint thinner) to remove dust from recessed mouldings and other awkward corners.

FILLING DEFECTS IN WOOD

1 Fill splits and dents in wood using filler (spackle) on painted surfaces, and tinted wood stopper (patcher) on new or stripped wood that will be varnished.

2 Use the corner of a filling knife (putty knife), or even a finger, to work the wood filler into recesses and other awkward-to-reach places. Smooth off excess filler before it dries.

3 When the filler or wood stopper has hardened completely, use abrasive paper (sandpaper) wrapped around a sanding block to sand the repair down flush.

FILLING CRACKS IN PLASTER

1 Use the corner of a filling knife (putty knife) to rake out loose material along the line of the crack, and to undercut the edges slightly so that the filler has a better grip.

2 Brush out dust and debris from the crack, using an old paintbrush. Alternatively, use the crevice nozzle attachment of a vacuum cleaner.

3 Dampen the surrounding plaster with water from a garden spray gun to prevent it from drying out the filler too quickly and causing it to crack.

4 Mix up some filler on a plasterer's hawk (mortarboard) or a board offcut to a firm consistency. Alternatively, use ready-mixed filler or wallboard compound.

5 Use a filling knife to press the filler well into the crack, drawing the blade across it and then along it. Aim to leave the repair slightly proud.

DEALING WITH STAINS

If ceilings have been stained by plumbing leaks, seal the affected area with a proprietary aerosol stain sealer to prevent the stain from showing through the new paint film. Alternatively, paint the affected area with white gloss (oil) paint – it will seal just as well and is usually already on hand. It can be overpainted with water-based (latex) paint.

6 When the filler has hardened, use fine-grade abrasive paper (sandpaper) wrapped around a sanding block to smooth the repair flush with the surrounding wall.

STRIPPING PAINT

Every time a surface is repainted, this adds a little more thickness to the paint layer. It does not matter much on wall or ceiling surfaces, but on woodwork (and, to a lesser extent, on metalwork) this build-up of successive layers of paint can eventually lead to the clogging of detail on mouldings. More importantly, moving parts such as doors and windows start to bind and catch against their frames. If this happens, it is time to strip off the paint back to bare wood and build up a new paint system from scratch.

It may also be necessary to strip an old paint finish if it is in such poor condition – from physical damage, for example – that repainting will no longer cover up the faults adequately.

There are two methods of removing paint from wood and metal surfaces. The first is using *heat*, traditionally from a blowtorch but nowadays more often an electric heat gun. The second is to use a *chemical paint remover*, which contains either dimethylene chloride or caustic soda. Heat works well on wood, but may scorch the surface and can crack the glass in windows; it is less successful on metal because the material conducts heat away as it is applied. Chemicals work well on all surfaces, but need handling with care; always follow the manufacturer's instructions to the letter.

HOMEMADE PASTE REMOVER

Add caustic soda to water until no more will dissolve. Thicken to a paste with oatmeal and use as for proprietary paste remover. Be particularly careful when using this corrosive solution. If it splashes on the skin, rinse at once with plenty of cold water.

USING A HEAT GUN

1 Play the air stream from the heat gun over the surface to soften the paint film. Scrape it off as it bubbles up, and deposit the hot scrapings in an old metal container.

2 Use a shavehook (triangular scraper) instead of a flat scraper to remove the paint from mouldings. Take care not to scorch the wood if it is to be varnished afterwards.

3 Remove any remnants of paint from the wood surface with wire wool soaked in white spirit (paint thinner), working along the direction of the grain.

4 Use a hand vacuum cleaner to remove any remaining loose particles of paint from the crevices in mouldings and from any other inaccessible areas.

5 Sand the surface of the wood lightly to remove any raised fibres or rough patches, then wipe it over with a clean cloth moistened with white spirit.

7 Apply a coat of either wood primer or a combined primer/ undercoat to the stripped wood surface to provide optimum adhesion for the subsequent top coats.

6 Seal the resin in any exposed knots by brushing on a coat of liquid knotting (shellac). Leave this to dry thoroughly before priming the wood.

USING LIQUID REMOVER

1 Wear rubber gloves and old clothing. Decant the liquid into a polythene (polyethylene) container or an old can, then brush it onto the surface you want to strip. Leave it until the paint film bubbles up.

2 Use a flat scraper or shavehook (triangular scraper) as appropriate to remove the softened paint. Deposit the scrapings safely in an old container.

3 Neutralize the stripper by washing the surface down with water or white spirit (paint thinner), as recommended by the manufacturer. Leave it to dry.

USING PASTE REMOVER

1 Paste removers are especially good for removing paint from intricate mouldings because they dry very slowly. Apply the paste liberally to the surface.

2 Give the paste plenty of time to work, especially on thick paint layers. Then scrape it off and wash down the surface with plenty of water to neutralize the chemical.

USING A PAINTBRUSH

The paintbrush is the most versatile and therefore the most widely used tool for applying paint. Choose the brush size to match the surface being painted. For example, for painting glazing bars (muntins) on windows or narrow mouldings on a door, use a slim brush – or perhaps a cutting-in (sash) brush if painting up to an adjacent unpainted surface such as glass where a neat edge to the paint film is needed. For expansive, flat areas select a larger brush for quick coverage. Remember that the largest wall brushes can be tiring to use, especially with solvent-based (oil) paints.

Get rid of any loose bristles in a new brush by flicking it vigorously across the palm of the hand before using it for the first time. Wash previously used brushes that have been stored unwrapped to remove any dust or other debris from the bristles, and leave them to dry out again before using them to apply a solvent-based paint.

Always check that the metal ferrule is securely attached to the brush handle, and hammer in any projecting nails or staples. Check too that the ferrule is free from rust which could discolour the paint. To remove rust use either wire wool or abrasive paper (sandpaper).

PREPARING THE PAINT

1 Wipe the lid first to remove any dust. Then prise it off with a wide lever such as the thicker edge of a table knife to avoid damage to the lip.

2 Decant some paint into a clean metal or plastic paint kettle, or small bucket. This is easier to handle than a full container, especially one without a handle.

3 Remove any paint skin from partly used containers. Then strain the paint into the paint kettle through a piece of old stocking or tights (pantyhose), or cheesecloth.

HOLDING THE BRUSH

1 Before using a new brush, work it vigorously backwards and forwards across the palm of the hand to remove any loose bristles. Wash brushes that have been stored for a while.

2 The best control of a small or medium-sized brush is achieved by holding it with the fingers and thumb on the ferrule, rather than on the handle.

3 Wide wall brushes can be tiring to use, and it is usually more comfortable to grip the brush by the handle rather than by the ferrule.

USING A BRUSH

1 To load the brush with paint, dip it into the paint to about a third of the bristle depth. An overloaded brush will cause drips, and paint will run down the brush handle.

2 Tie a length of string or wire across the mouth of the paint kettle between the handle supports, and use it to scrape excess paint from the bristles.

3 Apply the paint to the wood in long, sweeping strokes, brushing the paint out along the grain direction until the brush begins to run dry.

4 Load up the brush with more paint and apply it to the next area. Blend the two together with short, light strokes, again along the grain direction.

5 Repeat this process while working across the area, blending the edges of adjacent areas together with light brushstrokes to avoid leaving a visible join.

6 At edges and external corners, let the brush run off the edge to avoid a build-up of paint on the corner. Repeat the process for the opposite edge.

USING PAINT ROLLERS AND PADS

Paint rollers are generally used to apply water-based (latex) paints to large, flat areas such as walls and ceilings. Choose a sleeve with a short pile for painting plaster, a medium pile for painting embossed or textured wall coverings, and a long pile for deeply sculpted surfaces such as those created with textured finishes (texture paints). Rollers can also apply solvent-based (oil) paint to flat surfaces such as flush doors, but tend to leave a distinctive 'orange peel' texture rather than the smooth finish left by a paintbrush.

There are some drawbacks with paint rollers: they cannot paint right up to internal corners or wall/ceiling angles, so these need to be painted first with a brush or pad. They can also splash if 'driven' too fast, and the sleeves take a lot of time and effort to clean thoroughly, especially if they have been used for a long period and there is dried paint in the pile. Repeated cleaning eventually causes the sleeve to peel from its core.

People either love or loathe paint pads. They tend to apply less paint per coat than either a brush or a roller, so an additional coat may be needed in some circumstances, but they make it easy to apply paint smoothly and evenly with no risk of brush marks.

USING A ROLLER

1 Select a sleeve with the required fibre type and pile length, and slide it onto the sprung metal cage until it meets the stop next to the handle.

2 Decant some paint (previously strained if from an old can) into the roller tray until the paint level just laps up the sloping section.

3 Brush a band of paint about 50 mm (2 in) wide into internal corners and wall/ceiling angles, around doors and windows, and above skirtings (baseboards).

4 Load the roller sleeve with paint by running it down the sloping section into the paint. Then roll it up and down the slope to remove the excess.

5 Start applying the paint in a series of overlapping diagonal strokes to ensure complete coverage of the surface. Continue until the sleeve runs dry.

6 Reload the sleeve and tackle the next section in the same way. Finish off by blending the areas together, working parallel to corners and edges.

USING A PAINT PAD

2 On walls, apply the paint in a series of overlapping parallel bands. Use a small pad or a special edging pad (see step 4) to paint right up to corners or angles.

1 Pour some paint into the special applicator tray. Then load the pad by running it backwards and forwards over the ridged loading roller.

3 Use smaller pads for painting narrow areas such as mouldings on doors or glazing bars (muntins) on windows. Bush out the paint along the direction of the grain.

4 Special edging pads are designed for painting right up to internal angles, and have small wheels which guide the pad along the adjacent surface as you work.

USING AEROSOL PAINT

Aerosol paints and varnishes are ideal for hard-to-decorate surfaces such as wickerwork. Always follow the maker's instructions when using them.

5 Some larger pads can be fitted to an extension pole to make it easier to paint ceilings and high walls. Make sure the pad is attached securely.

PAINTING WALLS AND CEILINGS

Paint is a popular decorative finish for walls and ceilings because it is quick and easy to apply, offers a huge range of colours and is relatively inexpensive compared with rival products such as wall coverings. It can be used over plain plaster, or can be applied over embossed relief wall coverings and textured finishes.

Before starting painting, clear the room and prepare the surfaces. Start by taking down curtains and blinds (drapes and shades). Remove furniture to another room if possible, or else group it in the middle of the room and cover it with clear plastic sheeting. Take down lampshades and pendant light fittings (after turning off the power supply). Unscrew wall-mounted fittings and remove the hardware from doors and windows if they are being repainted at the same time.

Protect surfaces not being repainted, such as wall switches and socket outlets (receptacles), with masking tape. Finally, cover the floor with dust sheets (drop cloths), which will absorb paint splashes; vacuum-clean surfaces such as window sills, picture rails and skirtings (baseboards) where dust can settle, and turn off forced-air heating so that dust is not recirculated into the room.

Access equipment

Normally most of the surfaces to be painted can be reached from a standing or a kneeling position, but for ceilings, the tops of room walls and the upper reaches of stairwells some access equipment is needed. A simple stepladder, ideally with a top platform big enough to support a paint kettle or roller tray, will be adequate for painting walls and ceilings.

PAINTING WALLS AND CEILINGS

Paint walls and ceilings in a series of overlapping bands. Start painting the ceiling next to the window wall so that reflected light on the wet paint shows whether coverage is even. On walls, right-handed people should work from right to left, and left-handed people the other way.

For stairwells, use steps or ladder sections plus secured scaffold boards or the components of a slot-together access tower to set up a work platform that allows you to get to all the surfaces without over-reaching.

Texture paints

These are water-based (latex) paints thickened with added fillers. Once the paint has been applied to the decorating surface, a range of three-dimensional effects can be created using various patterning or texturing techniques. These paints are ideal for covering up surfaces in poor condition. Most are white, but they can be overpainted with ordinary water-based paint for a coloured effect. Avoid using this type of paint in kitchens as the textured surface will over time trap dirt and grease which makes the surface difficult to keep clean.

PAINT COVERAGE

Paint coverage depends on several factors, including the roughness and porosity of the surface to which it is being applied and the thickness of the coating. For example, the first coat of paint will soak into new plaster, so the coverage will be less than is achieved with subsequent coats. Similarly, a textured surface will hold more paint than a smooth one, again reducing the paint coverage.

The figures given here are intended as a rough guide only. Always check the manufacturer's coverage figure on the container, and use that plus the area to be painted to work out how much paint is required.

ESTIMATING QUANTITIES

Paint type	Sq m per litre	Sq ft per gallon
Liquid gloss (oil) paint	16	650
Non-drip gloss paint	13	530
Eggshell	12	490
Matt (flat) water-based (latex) paint	15	610
Silk (satin) water-based paint	14	570
Non-drip water-based paint	12	490
Undercoat	11	450
Wood primer	12	490
Metal primer	10	410
Varnish	15–20	610–820

USING TEXTURE PAINT

1 Start applying the paint to the wall or ceiling surface in a series of overlapping random strokes, recharging the roller or brush at intervals.

2 When an area of about 1 sq m (11 sq ft) is covered, go over the whole area with a series of parallel roller/brush strokes for an even surface texture.

3 Give the textured finish the look of tree bark by drawing a flat-bladed scraper or similar edged tool over the surface to flatten off the high spots.

4 Use a texturing comb to create overlapping swirls, working across the area. Practise the effect on paint applied to a piece of heavy cardboard first.

5 Twist a sponge before pulling it away from the wall surface to create a series of small, overlapping swirls in the paint finish. Rinse the sponge regularly.

6 You can buy patterning roller sleeves in a range of different designs for use with texture paints. This one creates a regular diamond pattern.

7 This patterning sleeve gives a random streaked effect when rolled down the wall. Apply the texture paint with a brush first if using a patterning sleeve.

PAINTING DOORS

The main problem with painting doors – or indeed any woodwork with a large surface area – involves keeping what professional decorators call a *wet edge*. Obviously the door has to be painted bit by bit, and if the edge of one area begins to dry before this is joined up to the next area, the join will show when the paint dries completely.

The secret of success is to work in a sequence, as shown in the accompanying drawings of flush and panelled doors, and to complete the job in one continuous operation, working as fast as reasonably possible.

Before starting to paint a door, wedge it open so there is room to walk through the doorway without touching wet paint, and also so that the hinged edge of the door can be reached easily. Remove handles, locks and other fittings; wedge a length of dowel in the latch hole to make a temporary handle for use until the paint has dried. Slide a dust sheet (drop cloth) underneath the door to catch any drips. Finally, warn everyone else in the house that the door is covered with wet paint, and keep children and pets out of the way in another room or out of doors.

PAINTING FLUSH DOORS

1 Remove the door furniture and wedge the door open. Then divide it up into eight or ten imaginary squares, and start painting at the top of the door by filling in the first square. Brush the paint out towards the door edges so it does not build up on the external angles.

2 Move on to the next block at the top of the door, brushing paint out towards the top and side edges as before. Carefully blend the two areas together with horizontal brushstrokes, then with light vertical laying-off strokes.

3 Continue to work down the door surface block by block, blending the wet edges of adjacent blocks together as they are painted. Always aim to complete a flush door in one session to prevent the joints between blocks showing up as hard lines. Replace the door furniture when the paint is touch-dry.

PAINTING PANELLED DOORS

1 Tackle panelled doors by painting the mouldings (**1**) around the recessed panels first. Take care not to let paint build up in the corners or to stray onto the faces of the cross-rails at this stage. Then paint the recessed panels (**2**).

2 Next, paint the horizontal cross-rails (**3**), brushing lightly inwards towards the painted panel mouldings to leave a sharp paint edge. Feather the paint out thinly where it runs onto the vertical stiles at each end of the rails.

3 Finish the door by painting the vertical centre rail (**4**) and the outer stiles (**5**), again brushing towards the panel mouldings. Where the rail abuts the cross-rails, finish with light brushstrokes parallel to the cross-rails.

PAINTING DOOR EDGES

Where the two faces of a door are being painted in two different colours, the convention is to match the colour of the hinged edge to that of the closing face of the door – the one facing the next room – and to paint the leading edge to match the other door face.

1 HINGED EDGE

VARNISHING WOOD

1 On bare wood, use a clean lint-free cloth to wipe the first coat onto the wood, working along the grain direction. This coat acts as a primer/sealer.

2 Sand the first coat lightly when dry to remove any 'nibs' caused by dust particles settling on the wet varnish, then wipe off the sanding dust.

3 Apply the second and subsequent coats of varnish with a brush, applying it along the grain and linking up adjacent areas with light brush strokes.

PAINTING WINDOWS

Windows are more difficult to paint than doors because they contain so many different surfaces, especially small-paned types criss-crossed with slim glazing bars (muntins). There is also the additional problem of paint straying onto the glass. The ideal is a neat paint line that covers the bedding putty and extends onto the glass surface by about 3 mm (1/8 in) to seal the joint and prevent condensation from running down between putty and glass.

With hinged windows, the edges of the casement or top opening light (transom) should be painted to match the colour used on the inside of the window. With double-hung sliding sash windows, the top and bottom edges of each sash and the top, bottom and sides of the frame are all painted to match the inner face of the sashes.

Remove the window hardware before you start painting. On casement windows tap a nail into the bottom edge of the casement and into the lower frame rebate and link them with stiff wire to stop the casement from swinging open or shut.

For best results, sash windows should be removed from their frames before painting. Modern spring-mounted windows are easy to release from their frames. With older cord-operated types, remove the staff beads (window stops) first to free the sashes. Although quite a major task, take the opportunity to renew the sash cords (pulley ropes). This makes it possible to cut the cords to free the window. Some making good and finishing off will have to be done after the window is reassembled.

PAINTING A CASEMENT WINDOW

1 Remove the window furniture from the opening casement and wedge the window open while you work. Tackle the glazing bars (muntins) and edge mouldings first (**1**), then the face of the surrounding casement frame (**2**) and finally the hinged edge of the casement. Paint the other edges from outside.

2 Move on to paint the glazing bars and edge mouldings (**3**) of the fixed casement. Use masking tape or a paint shield to ensure neat, straight edges here and on the opening casement; the paint should overlap the glass by about 3 mm (1/8 in). Paint the face of the surrounding casement frame (**4**).

PAINTING A SASH WINDOW

1 To paint sash windows without removing the sashes from their frames, start by raising the bottom (inner) sash and lowering the top (outer) one. Paint the lower half of the top sash (**1**), including its bottom edge, and the exposed parting beads at the top and bottom (**2**) and the exposed sides of the frame itself.

2 When the paint is touch-dry, reverse the sash positions and paint the upper half of the top sash (**3**), including its top edge, and the exposed and unpainted parting beads and frame sides (**4**).

PAINTING AROUND GLASS

3 Paint the outer frame (**5**), then the centre frame member between the opening and fixed casements (**6**). Complete the job by painting the window sill (**7**) and the rebate into which the opening casement closes.

1 Stick masking tape to the glass with its edge 3 mm (1/8 in) from the wood. Paint the surrounding wood, removing the tape when the paint is touch-dry.

2 Alternatively, hold a paint shield against the edge of the glazing bar (muntin) or surrounding moulding while painting. Wipe the shield regularly to prevent smears.

USING STAIN

3 Finish off by painting the face and edges of the inner sash (5), the staff beads and any other trim mouldings around the window (6). Finally, paint the window sill (7). Leave the sashes ajar until the paint has dried thoroughly to avoid components sticking.

Test the stain on an offcut of the same wood, or in an inconspicuous area. If necessary, dilute it. Use a clean lint-free cloth to apply stain to bare wood. If the result is too pale, apply further coats when the first is dry. Avoid overlapping parallel bands of stain; the overlap will show up as a darker area when the stain dries.

TIP

To clean up an untidy paint edge on the glass, use a ruler and a very sharp knife to cut a clean edge, and carefully scrape off the excess paint up to the cut line.

SPECIAL PAINT EFFECTS

There is no need to stick to plain colour on painted walls as there is a wide range of special paint effects that will enliven their looks. Some of these effects are purely decorative in their own right; others imitate the appearance of other materials. All can be created with the use of inexpensive tools and materials, and practice and patience will bring highly attractive results.

The special paint effects dealt with here fall into two broad groups: *broken colour* and *imitation*. In the first group a range of different techniques is used to apply a second colour over a different base colour so that the latter still shows through, providing a pleasing two-colour effect. In the second group paint is used to copy the looks of materials such as wood veneers and marble.

For either finish it is essential to prepare the surface of the wall or woodwork thoroughly first (see chart).

Glazes

Most special effects are applied as a tinted glaze which is semi-transparent and allows the underlying base colour to show through. Water-based glazes are made from water-based (latex) paint diluted with water or a proprietary emulsion glaze until the required level of translucency has been achieved. Use coloured paints or tint white paint to the required shade with artists' acrylics. Water-based glazes produce a thinner, more open, coat of colour and they dry extremely quickly, which means they are not suitable for the more complex special paint effects.

Scumble is the main component of solvent-based (oil) glazes and is generally diluted with a mixture of 1 part linseed oil to 2 parts white spirit (paint thinner). However, the proportions can be varied: a higher proportion of scumble will increase the definition of the effect and will retard the drying time; more linseed oil produces a smoother texture; white spirit thins the glaze and speeds up the drying time. Once the glaze has been mixed, pour off a small quantity and add the colour to this, using either eggshell paint or artists' oils. When the correct colour has been mixed, gradually add this to the main quantity of glaze until the required level of transparency is achieved. Solvent-based glazes have a rich, hardwearing

TOOLS AND MATERIALS

Among the tools and materials needed are a stencilling brush (**1**), a dusting brush (**2**), a small paintbrush (**3**), a softening brush (**4**), a stippling brush (**5**), artists' paintbrushes (**6**), cotton or linen rags (**7**), a natural marine sponge (**8**), a rubber rocker for graining (**9**), a large paintbrush (**10**) and a flat-bristle varnishing brush (**11**).

finish and the slower drying times are particularly suited to special effects.

If working over large areas – more than 2 sq m (22 sq ft) – two people will be needed to achieve the best finish: one to apply the glaze and the other to work it. This is the only way to maintain a wet edge and therefore to avoid noticeable joins between one area of colour and the next.

Stencilling

This is slightly different from the other techniques, since the stencil produces a clearly defined shape. It is very simple to do, and can be used to create effects in more than one colour by using different stencils. Ready-cut stencils can be bought, but it is easy to create designs of your own.

PREPARING SURFACES

The method of preparation varies depending on whether water-based (latex) paints or solvent-based (oil) paints are used for the final effect. Care taken at this early stage will help to ensure a satisfying end result.

Once the preparation is complete, apply the chosen base colour. Use eggshell for a good opaque and non-porous surface if using either a water- or a solvent-based finish and, when dry, rub it down with fine abrasive paper (sandpaper).

Surface	Water-based effect	Solvent-based effect
Bare plaster	Prime with diluted water-based paint	Prime with proprietary primer or PVA adhesive (white glue)
	Apply 1–2 water-based undercoats	Apply 1–2 solvent-based undercoats
Painted plaster	Wash down, repair defects and sand solvent-based finishes	Wash down, repair defects and sand solvent-based finishes
	Apply 1–2 water-based undercoats	Apply 1–2 solvent-based undercoats
Hardboard	Prime with diluted water-based paint	Prime with proprietary primer
	Apply 1–2 water-based undercoats	Apply 1–2 solvent-based undercoats
Bare wood	Apply knotting (shellac) to knots	Apply knotting (shellac) to knots
	Prime with diluted water-based paint	Apply proprietary primer
	Apply 1–2 water-based undercoats	Apply 1–2 solvent-based undercoats
Painted wood	As for Painted plaster	As for Painted plaster
Varnished wood	Strip and prepare as for Bare wood	Strip and prepare as for Bare wood

CUTTING STENCILS

To cut stencils, tracing paper, some special waxed paper for stencils (available from art stores), a pencil, a pin and a scalpel or sharp utility knife are needed. Trace or draw the pattern and enlarge or reduce it on a photocopier, if necessary. Tape the finished trace to the stencil paper and prick through it to mark the design outline on the stencil paper. Join up the prick marks in pencil. Alternatively, transfer the trace onto the stencil using carbon paper. Cut out the design carefully, leaving sufficient ties to bridge the separate areas of the design. Allow a large margin above and below the design so that the stencil is sufficiently strong. Reinforce any tears or accidental cuts with adhesive tape.

1 Affix the stencil to the surface with masking tape, aligning it with a true horizontal pencil guideline. Dip the stencilling brush in the paint and remove the excess on some waste paper. Use a pouncing action to apply the paint to minimize the risk of colour seeping under the stencil and marring the masked-off areas.

2 When the paint is touch-dry, release the stencil, wipe off the wet paint and reposition it farther along the wall to create the next section of the pattern.

SPECIAL PAINT
EFFECTS *(continued)*

Sponging

This technique involves dabbing irregular patches of paint onto the base coat. Two or more different sponged colours can be applied. Note that a natural marine sponge must be used to create this effect; man-made sponges do not work. Soak it in water first until it swells to its full size, then wring it out ready to start applying the paint.

1 After testing the effect on an offcut of board, dip the sponge in the paint and apply light pressure to leave overlapping splodges of colour.

2 Allow the first application to dry, then go over the surface again and add more colour if necessary to deepen the contrast with the base colour.

3 If applying a different second colour, allow the first colour to dry and then use the same technique to apply the new colour over it.

Rag-rolling

Another simple two-colour effect, rag-rolling involves brushing a diluted second colour over the base coat and then using a rolled-up 'sausage' of cloth to remove some of the second colour before it starts to dry.

The technique works best with a base coat of eggshell paint and a top coat of eggshell paint diluted with white spirit (paint thinner). Use lint-free cotton or linen rags and change them frequently before they become soaked with paint.

1 Allow the base coat to dry thoroughly. Then lightly brush on the second diluted colour in bands across the surface, aiming to leave a random pattern of brushstrokes that allows the base colour to show through.

2 Roll the rag sausage across the surface in a continuous motion. Vary the direction for a random effect and touch in small areas by just dabbing with the cloth. Replace the rag regularly.

Stippling

For an attractive mottled appearance, try stippling; apart from being used as a decorative finish in its own right it can also be used to obliterate brush marks in the base coat beneath other broken-colour effects.

The one item of specialist equipment that is needed to create this effect is a stippling brush.

1 Brush the glaze on over the base coat, applying a generous coat. Do not worry about leaving brush marks; the stippling will obliterate them.

2 Hold the stippling brush with the bristle tips parallel with the surface, and simply hit the paint film. Clean paint from the brush regularly, wiping it with a dry cloth.

Colour washing

This is one of the simplest broken-colour effects. Brush on the glaze and then use a dry softening brush or an ordinary wide paintbrush to create a random pattern of brushstrokes that allow the base coat to show through. A further colour can be added.

1 Brush a liberal coat of the glaze over the base coat. The effect of colour washing is enhanced when there is a good contrast between the two paint colours.

2 Draw the softening brush over the glaze in a series of long random strokes in varying directions. Add a further toning colour if desired when this coat has dried.

SPECIAL PAINT EFFECTS *(continued)*

Graining

Graining is a technique that aims to imitate the look of natural wood, especially the more exotic and expensive species. Use a solvent-based (oil) eggshell paint for the base coat, and a solvent-based glaze.

2 Then, after a couple of minutes, draw a dry graining brush or an ordinary paintbrush lightly over the glaze to create the actual grain pattern.

3 Use a rubber rocker (above), a graining comb or a bristle grainer to produce the individual grain characteristics of the wood you are copying.

1 Brush the glaze onto the wood surface, leaving the brush marks visible along the direction of the intended wood grain.

Dragging

Another very simple effect, dragging is created by drawing a dry brush over the glaze in a series of parallel strokes that allow the base colour to show through. Use a normal paintbrush in a width to suit the surface being decorated.

1 Brush a generous coat of glaze over the base coat. Always work parallel to the direction of the grain if applying the effect to wood.

2 Use a dry paintbrush to drag a series of parallel lines in the second colour. Wipe the build-up of paint off the brush at regular intervals with a dry cloth.

Marbling

As its name implies, marbling copies the appearance of marble. It is a relatively difficult technique to master, but the results can be quite spectacular. For a first attempt choose a piece of real marble to copy. For best results work with a solvent-based (oil) glaze, applied over an eggshell base coat. Add the veining details with artists' oils.

1 Either brush out the glaze or apply it with a pad of lint-free cloth. Only a relatively thin coat is needed.

2 Use a dusting brush as here or a stippling brush to stipple the surface of the wet glaze. Add more colour to the glaze mixture, apply selectively to some areas for contrast and stipple the glaze again.

3 Working on the wet glaze, draw in the main areas of veining with an artists' paintbrush and a mixture of glaze and artists' oils. Use different weights of line to create a natural-looking effect.

4 Use the softening brush again to soften the outlines of the veining and to blend it into the background. Wipe the brush regularly to avoid smudges.

VARNISHING SPECIAL PAINT EFFECTS

Some special paint effects, especially graining and marbling, should be sealed with a coat of clear varnish once the effect has dried completely. Use satin varnish rather than gloss unless a particularly polished effect is required. When this has dried, burnish the surface with a soft cloth and add a little wax polish to create a realistic surface sheen, if wished.

5 Highlight some areas of the veining by adding more colour or a second colour. Soften the effect again, as in step 4.

PAPERHANGING

The term 'wall coverings' is used to describe the whole range of decorative materials sold in roll form and designed to be stuck to wall and ceiling surfaces with a strippable adhesive. The range includes an enormous variety of designs, patterns and colourways … almost too many, as any home decorator will testify when confronted by an array of pattern books and trying to decide which covering to select.

The vast majority of wall coverings are either made entirely from paper, or have a plastic or cloth layer bonded to a paper backing so that they can be hung in the same way as all-paper types. The basic technology of paperhanging has changed little over the centuries, even if the products have been subtly altered and improved; people still paper the living room in a way that would be familiar to their grandparents.

The two main developments that have occurred in recent years are the introduction of ready-pasted types which are immersed in a trough of water instead of having paste brushed onto them, and of all-plastic wall coverings which are hung by pasting the wall.

This chapter gives information on the various types of wall covering available and on the tools, materials and other equipment needed to hang or strip them. There is advice on how to go about removing existing wall decorations – other wall coverings, materials such as texture paints, wall panelling and tiles of various types – and on preparing the surface. This is followed by detailed step-by-step instructions on how to hang a new wall covering on walls and ceilings, and on how to cope with awkward areas such as door and window openings, arches and stairwells.

Opposite: There is virtually no limit to the versatility of modern wall coverings. This complementary match of broken colour and simple stripes is linked by a striking multicoloured border at dado (chair) rail level.

TYPES OF WALL COVERING

Wall coverings fall into two basic groups: those with a printed design or a surface material which is decorative in its own right, and those with a surface texture or embossing which are designed to be painted over once they have been hung.

Printed wallpaper is exactly that – paper with a coloured design printed on it. It may also be embossed along the lines of the design, or may have a distinctive surface texture added during manufacture. Cheaper types may be awkward to hang, tearing easily or stretching so as to make accurate pattern matching difficult. More expensive types, especially hand-printed ones, are better in this respect, but care must still be taken when hanging them to keep paste off the face of the paper. The strongest printed wallpapers are called *duplex papers*, and are made by bonding two layers of paper together during the manufacturing process. Most printed papers can be wiped with a damp cloth if they become stained, but it is wise to check whether this is the case when selecting this type of wall covering. All are easy to strip, making them a good choice if you like to redecorate regularly.

Washable wallpaper is a printed wallpaper which has a thin clear plastic coating applied over the design during manufacture to render it water and stain resistant. As with printed types, the surface may be embossed or textured. Washable wallpapers are also widely available in ready-pasted form. The plastic surface will withstand gentle washing and sponging with a mild detergent, but not prolonged scrubbing or the use of abrasive cleaners. Choose them for rooms where they will be subject to moderate wear, or for steamy conditions such as are

Above: Contrasting wall coverings can help to change the proportions of a room. Here a darker wall covering helps lower the ceiling.

Left: Stencil borders with the design printed on a clear self-adhesive backing allow the wall covering beneath to show through – the perfect solution for unwilling stencillers.

When hanging a ready-pasted wall covering, the table, bucket and brush can be dispensed with. All that is needed is a plastic soaking trough in which to immerse the rolled-up lengths of wall covering.

Before starting hanging, a plumb bob and line are needed to mark a true vertical line on the wall against which to hang the first length.

Most wall coverings are applied with a special soft-bristled paperhanging brush. These are generally between 190 and 250 mm (7¹/₂ to 10 in) wide, and have a slim handle. The soft bristles help to make the wall covering follow the contours of the wall surface behind, and also eliminate undue hand contact with the face of the covering, which might mark it.

A sponge can be used instead of a brush for hanging washables or vinyls, especially if they are ready-pasted, since here the sponge helps mop water from the surface of the wall covering as well as smoothing it into place.

The final stage is trimming, and the best tool for this is a special pair of paperhangers' scissors. These have blades up to 300 mm (12 in) long for making long, straight cuts.

For papering walls a stepladder is needed which should be tall enough to enable the ceiling to be easily touched. For papering ceilings, set up a proper platform across the width of the room at a comfortable height, using scaffold boards or staging on trestles or other low supports to ensure complete stability. Do not step from chair to chair or set up similar makeshift arrangements.

PASTING TABLES

A flat surface is needed to lay the paper on while it is being pasted. It is best to use a proper pasting table. This is a lightweight folding table covered in hardboard or plywood on a softwood frame, and is usually about 1.8 m (6 ft) long and just wider than a standard roll of wall covering. If you cannot buy, borrow or hire a pasting table, one can be improvised by cutting a standard sheet of plywood or chipboard (particle board) down to the same width and supporting it on trestles or sawhorses.

SEAM ROLLERS

For smooth wall coverings, a tool called a seam roller can be used to make sure that the seams are well bonded to the wall. Do not use a seam roller on textured or embossed wall coverings, though, as it will flatten the embossing.

Displayed on a fold-up pasting table are a soaking trough (**1**), rubber gloves (**2**), sponge (**3**), pencil (**4**), sharp utility knife (**5**), paperhangers' scissors (**6**), plumb bob and line (**7**), retractable steel tape measure (**8**), steel straightedge (**9**), paste bucket (**10**), pasting brush (**11**), packet of ready-mixed paste (**12**), seam roller (**13**) and paperhanging brush (**14**). A spirit level (**15**) can do double duty in checking verticals and as a straightedge.

PREPARING FOR PAPERHANGING

Unrestricted access is a must for paperhanging. If working on just the walls, move all the furniture to the centre of the room and cover it with dust sheets (drop cloths). When tackling the ceiling too, it is best to remove all the furniture completely if there is space to store it elsewhere in the house; otherwise group it at one end of the room so that most of the ceiling can be done, and then move it to the other end to complete the job.

Next, take down curtains and blinds (drapes and shades) and remove wall-mounted or ceiling-mounted tracks. Turn off the electricity supply at the mains, then disconnect and remove wall or ceiling light fittings as necessary, covering the bare wire ends thoroughly with insulating tape before restoring the power supply to the rest of the house. In the USA, ceiling roses, wall switch plates and socket outlets can be unscrewed and removed without

disconnecting the wall receptacles or switches. Isolate, drain, disconnect and remove radiators, and unscrew their wall brackets. Call in a professional electrician or plumber for these jobs if unsure of how to do them safely.

Lift down pictures, and remove other wall-mounted fittings such as shelves and display units. To make it easy to relocate the screw holes afterwards, push a matchstick (wooden match) into each one (see Tip).

CHOOSING THE STARTING POINT

Above: Start paperhanging at the centre of a chimney breast (fireplace projection) if the wall covering has a large, dominant pattern. Otherwise start next to the door so the inevitable pattern break can be disguised above it.

Right: Work outwards from the centre of a dormer window so the design is centred on the window recess.

ESTIMATING WALL COVERINGS (WALLS)

Height	Distance around room																			
	9m 30ft	10m 33ft	12m 40ft	13m 42ft	14m 46ft	15m 50ft	16m 52ft	17m 56ft	19m 62ft	20m 66ft	21m 69ft	22m 72ft	23m 75ft	25m 82ft	26m 85ft	27m 88ft	28m 92ft	30m 98ft	
2.15–2.30 m/7–7^1/$_2$ ft	4	5	5	6	6	7	7	8	8	9	9	10	10	11	12	12	13	13	
2.30–2.45 m/7^1/$_2$–8 ft	5	5	6	6	7	7	8	8	9	9	10	10	11	11	12	13	13	14	
2.45–2.60 m/8–8^1/$_2$ ft	5	5	6	7	7	8	9	9	10	10	11	12	12	13	14	14	15	15	
2.60–2.75 m/8^1/$_2$–9 ft	5	5	6	7	7	8	9	9	10	10	11	12	12	13	14	14	15	15	
2.75–2.90 m/9–9^1/$_2$ ft	6	6	7	7	8	9	9	10	10	11	12	12	13	14	14	15	15	16	
2.90–3.05 m/9^1/$_2$–10 ft	6	6	7	8	8	9	10	10	11	12	12	13	14	14	15	16	16	17	
3.05–3.20 m/10–10^1/$_2$ ft	6	7	8	8	9	10	10	11	12	13	13	14	15	16	16	17	18	19	

Numbers are based on a standard roll size of 10.05 m (33 ft) long and 520 mm (20^1/$_2$ in) wide. The measurement around the room includes all windows and doorway.

If the walls and ceiling are at present painted, they need washing down to remove dirt, grease, smoke stains and the like. If they are decorated with another wall covering, this will have to be removed and any defects in the surface put right. Finally, they need sizing – treating with a diluted coat of wallpaper adhesive to even out the porosity of the surface and to help to improve the 'slip' of the pasted wall covering during hanging.

Measuring up

The next job is to estimate how many rolls of wall covering will be needed to decorate the room. If using a material that comes in standard-sized rolls, simply measure the room dimensions and refer to the charts given here for the number of rolls needed to cover the walls and ceiling. They allow for a typical door and window area; fewer rolls are needed for a room with large picture windows or wide door openings. If using a paper-backed cloth covering which comes in a nonstandard width, measure up each wall, and ask the supplier to estimate what length of material you will need; such materials

are too expensive to waste. Wall coverings in the USA vary in width and length but are usually available in rolls sized to cover a specified area, allowing for trimming.

Buying wall coverings

Wall coverings are made in batches, with a number printed on the label, and it is important to check that there are

sufficient rolls with the same batch number; colours may not match exactly between batches.

When hanging a wall covering with a particularly large pattern repeat, wastage is often unusually high and it may be wise to purchase one or two extra rolls, over and above the numbers given in the charts. Most suppliers will take back unopened rolls.

ESTIMATING WALL COVERINGS (CEILINGS)

Distance around room		No of
m	ft	rolls
10	33	2
11	36	2
12	40	2
13	42	3
14	46	3
15	50	4
16	52	4
17	56	4
18	59	5
19	62	5
20	66	5
21	69	6
22	72	7
23	75	7

TIP

Insert a matchstick (wooden match) in each hole left when unscrewing wall-mounted fixtures and fittings that will be replaced later. It will burst through the wall covering as this is applied and make it easy to find the screw holes.

STRIPPING OLD WALL COVERINGS

In the days when ordinary printed wall coverings were all that were usually on sale, it was common practice to paper over existing wallpaper, often to the point where four or five successive layers would accumulate. This is no longer considered acceptable (and will not work at all over today's washable and vinyl wall coverings), and it is always best to strip all old coverings before hanging new ones. Even if the old material looks sound, hanging a newly-pasted wall covering over it may cause it to lift from the wall, creating ugly bubbles that are impossible to disguise. This also applies to the backing paper that is left on the wall after dry-stripping a vinyl wall covering; there is no guarantee that it is perfectly bonded to the wall, and so hanging another wall covering over it could give very poor results.

Once the room is cleared and dust sheets (drop cloths) are spread over the floor and any remaining furniture, the next step is to identify what type of wall covering is to be removed. An ordinary printed paper will absorb water splashed on it immediately; other types will not. To tell washables from vinyls, pick and lift a corner and try to strip the wall covering dry. The printed plastic layer of a vinyl wall covering will peel off dry, but the surface of a washable paper will not come off in the same way unless it is a duplex paper made in two layers. With paper-backed fabric wall coverings, it is often possible to peel the fabric away from its paper backing; try it before turning to other more complicated methods of removal.

1 To strip printed wallpapers, wet the surface with a sponge or a garden spray gun. Wait for the water to penetrate, and repeat if necessary.

2 Using a stiff wallpaper scraper – not a filling knife (putty knife) – start scraping the old paper from the wall at a seam. Wet it again while working if necessary.

3 Turn off the power before stripping around switches and other fittings, then loosen the faceplate screws to strip the wallpaper behind them.

4 After removing the bulk of the old wallpaper, go back over the wall surface and remove any remaining 'nibs' of paper with sponge/spray gun and scraper.

5 To strip a washable wallpaper, start by scoring the plastic coating with a serrated scraper or toothed roller to allow the water to penetrate, then soak and scrape as before.

6 For quicker results, use a steam stripper to remove washable papers. Press the steaming plate to the next area while stripping the area just steamed.

STRIPPING VINYLS

1 Strip vinyl wall coverings by lifting a corner to separate the vinyl layer from the paper backing. Strip it off by pulling it away from the wall surface.

2 Always soak and remove the plain backing paper left on the wall after stripping a vinyl. It may well not be a sound lining for a new wall covering.

REMOVING OTHER OLD FINISHES

If the wall or ceiling to be given a new covering is painted or wallpapered, preparing the surface for its new finish is quite straightforward. However, if it was previously covered with materials such as texture paint, ceramic or polystyrene tiles or wall panelling, more work will be needed to remove the old finishes and return the surface to its original condition.

Textured finishes are tackled in different ways, depending on their type. Texture paints are basically thick water-based (latex) paints, normally used to create relatively low-relief effects, and can be removed with specially formulated paint removers. Some textured effects formed with a powder or ready-mixed compound are best removed with a steam wallpaper stripper, which softens the compound so that it can be scraped from the wall.

Never attempt to sand off a textured finish. There are two reasons. The first is that it will create huge quantities of very fine dust; the second is that older versions of this product contained asbestos fibres as a filler, and any action that might release these into the atmosphere as inhalable dust must be avoided at all costs.

For tiles and wall panelling, complete removal or a cover-up with plasterboard (gypsum board) are the two options available. The former will leave a surface in need of considerable renovation, while the latter will cause a slight loss of space within the room, as well as some complications at door and window openings.

REMOVING TEXTURED FINISHES

1 Strip texture paint by brushing on a generous coat of a proprietary texture paint remover. Stipple it well into the paint and leave it to penetrate.

2 When the paint has softened, scrape it off with a broad-bladed scraper. Wear gloves, and also safety goggles if working on a ceiling.

3 Once the bulk of the coating is removed, use wire wool dipped in the paint remover to strip off any remaining flecks of paint.

4 Remove powder-based or ready-mixed types using a steam stripper, which will soften the finish. Never try to sand off this type of finish.

REMOVING CERAMIC TILES

1 On a completely tiled wall, use a hammer to crack a tile and create a starting point for the stripping. On partly tiled walls, start at the tile edge.

2 Use a broad bolster (stonecutter's) chisel and a club (spalling) hammer to chip the old tiles off the wall. Have the wall replastered afterwards rather than trying to patch the surface up.

REMOVING POLYSTYRENE TILES

1 Lever the tiles away from the ceiling with a scraper. If they were fixed with a continuous coat of adhesive, consider covering the tiles with heavy lining paper as a temporary measure. For the best finish, fit a new plasterboard (gypsum board) ceiling, nailing through the tile layer into the joists.

2 If the tiles were fixed in place with blobs of adhesive, use a heat gun to soften the old adhesive so it can be removed with a broad-bladed scraper.

REMOVING WALL PANELLING

1 The last board to be fixed will have been nailed to the fixing grounds through its face. Use a nail punch to drive the nails in and free the board.

2 The other boards will have been secret-nailed through their tongues. Use a crowbar (wrecking bar) to prise them away from their grounds.

3 Finally, prise the grounds off the wall, and use a claw hammer or crowbar with some protective packing to lever the fixing nails out of the wall.

PREPARING SURFACES FOR COVERING

Once the previous wall and ceiling decorations have been removed the next task is to restore any defects in the surfaces to be covered, and then to prepare them so that they present the perfect substrate for successful paperhanging.

The first step is to put down some heavy-duty plastic sheeting on the floor to catch splashes, and then to wash down the bare wall and ceiling surfaces thoroughly with strong household detergent or sugar soap (all-purpose cleaner), working from the bottom up on walls, and then to rinse them off with clean water, working this time from top to bottom on walls. Turn off the electricity supply first in case water gets into light switches and socket outlets (receptacles). Leave the surfaces to dry out thoroughly.

Next, repair defects such as cracks, holes and other surface damage which may have been concealed by the previous decorations, or even caused by their removal.

Finally, treat the wall and ceiling surfaces with a coat of size or diluted wallpaper paste, and leave this to dry before starting paperhanging. Size seals porous plaster, providing a surface with even absorption, and also makes it easier to slide the pasted lengths of wall covering into position on the wall.

PREPARING WALLS AND CEILINGS

1 Wash wall surfaces down with sugar soap (all-purpose cleaner) or detergent, working from the bottom up, then rinse them with clean water, working from the top down.

2 Wash ceilings with a floor mop or squeegee, after disconnecting and removing light fittings. Again, rinse off with clean water.

3 Fill cracks, holes and other defects in the wall and ceiling surfaces as appropriate, leave the filler to harden and then sand the repair down flush.

4 Apply a coat of size or diluted wallpaper paste to wall and ceiling surfaces that are to be papered, and leave them to dry before starting paperhanging.

CROSS-LINING

If the wall surface is in poor condition, has been previously decorated with gloss paint or is being decorated with a thin fabric wall covering, it is best to hang lining (liner) paper first. This is usually hung horizontally rather than vertically, with butt joints between lengths and with ends and edges trimmed just short of adjacent ceiling and wall surfaces. Use the same type of paste for the lining paper as for the subsequent wall covering.

MEASURING AND CUTTING TO LENGTH

1 For quick and easy calculations, mark the whole length of the pasting table at 300 mm (12 in) intervals with a pencil and metal straightedge.

2 Measure the length of wall covering needed for the drop, including trim allowances, and mark this on the paper. Cut the first piece to length.

PASTING WALL COVERINGS

1 Face the light to make it easy to spot any unpasted areas – they look dull, not shiny. Apply a generous band of paste down the centre of the length.

2 Align one edge of the wall covering with the edge of the pasting table, then brush the paste out towards that edge from the centre band.

3 Draw the length across to the other edge of the table, and apply paste out to that edge too. Check that there are no dry or thinly pasted areas.

4 Continue pasting until the end of the table is reached. Then lift the pasted end of the wall covering and fold it over on itself, pasted side to pasted side.

5 Slide the paper along the table so the folded section hangs down. Paste the rest of the length and fold the other end over on itself as before.

HANGING THE FIRST LENGTHS

The first length of wall covering must be hung correctly if the decoration of the rest of the room is to go according to plan. Therefore the first thing to do is to decide on exactly where this is to be hung. The usual starting point is close to the door, just less than the wall covering's width away from the frame, so that the inevitable pattern discontinuity that will occur on returning to the starting point can be concealed on the short join above the door. If using a wall covering with a large design motif in a room which has a chimney breast (fireplace projection) it is preferable to start paperhanging on the chimney breast itself so that the design can be centred on it. When papering only part of a room, the starting point should be just less than the width of the wall covering from one corner of the room, to allow the edge of the covering to be trimmed accurately into the corner angle.

Next, use a roll of wall covering as a yardstick and mark off successive widths round the room walls with a pencil to check that there will not be any joins on external corners such as the sides of window reveals. If these occur, move the starting point along by about 50 mm (2 in) and recheck the join positions all round.

Finally, mark a true vertical line on the wall at the chosen starting point, using a pencil and a plumb bob and line. Failure to do this could result in the pattern running seriously out of true as successive lengths are hung.

1 At the chosen starting point, use a plumb bob and line to mark a vertical line on the wall surface. Join up the pencil marks with a straightedge.

2 Fetch the first length of pasted wall covering after leaving it to soak for the time recommended on the label. Carry it draped over the arm.

6 Peel the end of the length away from the wall so the excess can be trimmed with scissors. Brush the end back into place. Repeat at the bottom.

3 Unfold the upper flap and press the top edge of the length against the wall. Slide it across the wall until the edge lines up with the marked line.

4 Use a paperhanging brush (or a sponge for washables and vinyls) to smooth the wall covering into place. Work from the middle out towards the edges.

5 Use a pencil or the curved back of paperhanging scissors blades to mark the trimming line at ceiling level. Do the same at floor level.

TIP

7 Hang the next drop with the lengths exactly edge to edge. Brush the wall covering into the wall/ceiling angle and into the internal angle.

8 On flat wall coverings, run a seam roller down the join to ensure that it sticks securely. Never use a seam roller on embossed or relief wall coverings.

If a seam refuses to lie flat because it was inadequately pasted and has begun to dry out, brush a little extra paste underneath it and roll it again.

PAPERHANGING AROUND CORNERS

In a perfect world, rooms would have corners that were truly square and truly vertical, and it would be possible to hang wall covering all around the room in a continuous operation, simply turning the lengths that ran into the room corners straight onto the adjoining walls. In reality, corners are seldom square or true, and if the covering was hung in this way, lengths would be vertical on the first wall but could be running well off the vertical by the time they returned to the starting point. The effect can be visually disastrous, with vertical pattern elements clearly out of alignment at corners and horizontal pattern features sloping relative to the ceiling or skirting (baseboard).

The way to avoid these problems is to complete each wall with a cut-down strip that only just turns onto the next wall, to conceal the join in the corner angle. Then hang the remainder of the strip with its machine-cut edge against a newly drawn vertical line on the second wall, so that its other edge can be trimmed to follow the internal angle precisely. Any slight pattern discontinuity that results will not be noticeable except to the closest scrutiny, and the remaining lengths on the second wall will be hung truly vertically. A similar process is used when paperhanging around external corners, as at window reveals and on chimney breasts (fireplace projections).

PAPERING INTERNAL CORNERS

1 Hang the last full length before the corner of the room, then measure the distance to the corner from the edge of the length and add about 12 mm (1/2 in).

2 Use a pencil and straightedge to mark a strip of the required width, measured from the relevant edge (here, the left one), and cut it from the length.

3 Paste the strip and hang it in the usual way, allowing the hand-cut edge to lap onto the adjoining wall. Trim the top and bottom edges as usual.

4 Brush the tongue into the internal angle. If it will not lie flat because the corner is out of true, make small release cuts in the edge and brush it flat.

HANGING SPECIALITY WALL COVERINGS

1 Cut the wall covering to the length required, including a trim allowance, and roll it up face inwards around a broom handle or similar object.

2 Apply the recommended paste (usually a thick ready-mixed type) to the wall, and then unroll the wall covering onto the wet paste against a marked line.

3 Run a clean, dry paint roller backwards and forwards over the surface of the wall covering to bond it firmly to the wall.

4 Use a sharp utility knife – and a straightedge if needed – to trim the wall covering where it meets the ceiling and the skirting (baseboard).

5 To create neat joins, overlap adjoining lengths slightly and then cut through both layers with a sharp utility knife run along a straightedge.

6 Peel away the two waste strips and smooth the cut edges neatly back into place. Run a seam roller along the seam to ensure a good bond.

PUTTING UP FRIEZES AND BORDERS

Friezes and borders are narrow strips of printed paper or vinyl wall covering sold in rolls, and often come in colours and designs that complement wall coverings and fabrics manufactured by the same firm. A frieze is usually applied as a horizontal band running around the room, and can be positioned at ceiling level or next to a picture rail or dado (chair) rail. Borders, on the other hand, are used either to frame features of the room such as a door or window opening, or to create decorative panels on wall or ceiling surfaces – perhaps to frame a group of pictures, for example. They come in a range of widths.

Friezes and borders are available in plain and self-adhesive versions. The former is pasted in the same way as an ordinary wall covering, so this type is ideal for use on walls that have been painted or decorated with a plain printed wallpaper. If a border or frieze is to go over a washable or vinyl wall covering, use a special overlap adhesive or choose a self-adhesive type since ordinary wallpaper paste will not stick to the surface of the covering. Simply cut these to length, then peel off the backing paper bit by bit while positioning the length on the wall.

TIP

To gauge the effect a frieze or border will have, and to decide on the best position for it, stick lengths to the wall surface with masking tape before fixing them up permanently.

APPLYING A FRIEZE

1 Decide on the precise position of the frieze or border, then measure the distance from a nearby feature such as a ceiling or door frame.

2 Use a spirit level and pencil to draw true horizontal and vertical guidelines on the wall or ceiling surface at the marked position.

3 Cut the frieze or border to length and carefully apply paste to the length. Fold the paper up concertina fashion while working along the length.

4 Offer the free end of the concertina up to the marked line and brush it into place. It will help to have an assistant when hanging long lengths.

5 Join successive lengths end to end when starting a new roll. If the pattern does not match, overlap the ends so it does and cut through both layers.

6 Finally, check that all horizontal edges and vertical joints are well bonded to the wall by running over them with a seam roller. Remove excess paste.

APPLYING A BORDER

1 Put up the individual lengths of a border in the same way as a frieze. To form corners, overlap the lengths at right angles and cut through both layers at 45°.

2 Peel away the two waste sections and press the neatly mitred ends back into place. Adjust their positions if necessary to get a perfect joint.

3 The finished corner joint shows how accurate alignment and careful cutting result in a neat joint with the pattern meeting along the mitred cuts.

TILING

Tiles have a long pedigree in the interior decoration business. Faience (glazed earthenware) plaques have been found in Cretan buildings dating from around 1800 BC, and a tradition of ceramic wall and floor decoration was established soon after this farther east in Syria and Persia (now Iran). Mosaic wall and floor decorations, incorporating stone (usually marble), glass and ceramic tesserae, were also a major feature of Roman interiors. The technique spread to North Africa and thence to Spain, and the Renaissance soon led to widespread use of decorative tiling all over Europe.

Probably the most important centre of ceramic tile making in Europe was Holland, where the creation of individually handpainted tiles in a unique blue-grey colour soon made Delft famous in the early seventeenth century. From there, the use of tiles spread rapidly, and it was not long before mass production was introduced. The end product is the familiar ceramic tile we use today. The manufacturing and printing technology may have changed, and the adhesives and grouts used may have improved, but the result would be familiar to a seventeenth-century Dutchman.

The twentieth century has brought new kinds of tile, notably vinyl, lino and cork tiles which owe their existence to advances in plastics and resins technology. They offer a combination of properties that make them useful alternatives to ceramics in a wide range of situations, and are generally much less expensive.

This chapter concentrates on working with ceramic wall tiles, since they are the most popular of the types available. A wide range of situations is dealt with, from splashbacks to whole walls, including information on working around obstacles such as door and window openings and on creating special effects with tiled borders and feature panels. There are also sections on using other types of wall tiles, and on tiling floors.

Opposite: Wall tiles have never been available in such a profusion of styles and designs, ranging from highly glazed plain types to more rustic versions with matt or textured surfaces and patterns that look as though they have been handpainted.

TYPES OF WALL AND FLOOR TILES

Ceramic tiles provide the most durable of all finishes in the home, whether for walls, floors or worktops, and there has never been a bigger choice of colours, designs, shapes and sizes. The main drawback with tiles is that they are comparatively expensive, so it is important to make the right choice of tiles at the start, and to make sure that they are expertly fixed in place.

Vinyl, lino and cork floor tiles offer an alternative floor finish to ceramics, and offer the same advantages of ease of laying small units combined with a surface finish that is warmer to the touch and also less noisy underfoot than ceramic tiles.

Ceramic tiles for walls

In today's homes, the surfaces that are tiled more often than any other are walls, especially in rooms such as kitchens and bathrooms where a hardwearing, water-resistant and easy-to-clean decorative finish is required. Often the tiling protects only the most vulnerable areas such as splashbacks above wash basins and shower cubicles; but sometimes the whole room is tiled from floor to ceiling.

Tiles used for wall decoration are generally fairly thin, measuring from 4 to 6 mm (^{3}/16 to ^{1}/4 in) thick, although some imported tiles (especially the larger sizes) may be rather thicker than

Above: One of the most striking tiling effects is the feature panel (**top**), a group of tiles that builds up into a complete picture and looks particularly effective when framed with a border. Tiles set at 45° and interspersed with triangular cut tiles (**above**) can also add interest to the finished design.

Left: Many tile ranges include a variety of plain and patterned field tiles, teamed up with a complementary border tile, allowing the home decorator complete freedom to decide on the final design.

Right: Encaustic tiles are still made today using traditional materials and techniques. Unlike ordinary tiles, the pattern runs through the tile to form a very hardwearing decorative surface, ideal for hallways.

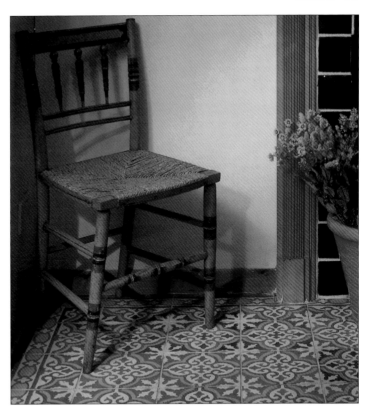

this. The commonest kinds are square, measuring 108 mm (4^1/4 in) or 150 mm (6 in) across, but rectangular tiles measuring 200 × 100 mm (8 × 4 in) and 200 × 150 mm (8 × 6 in) are becoming more popular.

Tile designs change with fashions in interior design, and current demand seems to be mainly for large areas of neutral or small-patterned tiles interspersed with individual motif tiles on a matching background. Plain tiles, often with a simple border frame, are also popular, as are tiles which create a frieze effect when laid alongside one another. Some sets of tiles build up into larger designs (known as feature panels), which can look quite striking when surrounded by an area of plain tiling. Some tile ranges still include what are known as *insert tiles* – tiles carrying moulded bathroom accessories

Above: Highly glazed tiles can make an unusual and durable surface for counter tops, but the grout lines need scrupulous cleaning to keep them hygienic.

such as soap dishes and toilet roll holders, though these are not as common or as popular as they were.

The surface of ceramic wall tiles is no longer always highly glazed, as it traditionally was. There are now semi-matt finishes, often with a slight surface texture that softens the somewhat harsh glare of a high-gloss surface.

Tile edges have changed over the years too. Once special round-edged tiles were used for the exposed edges of tiled areas, and plain ones with unglazed square edges (known as *field tiles*) elsewhere. Nowadays tiles are either the universal type or the standard square-edged variety. The former have angled edges so that when butted together they leave a gap for the grouting, which fills the spaces between them. The latter, as their name suggests, have square edges and so must be positioned with the aid of spacers.

Both types usually have two adjacent edges glazed so they can be used as perimeter tiles, and sometimes all four edges are glazed.

Tiles for floors and worktops

Although less widely used than wall tiles, ceramic floor tiles are a popular choice for heavy traffic areas such as porches and hallways. They are generally thicker and harder-fired than wall tiles, to enable them to stand up to heavy wear without cracking. Again, a wide range of plain colours, simple textures and more elaborate designs is available. Common sizes are 150 mm (6 in) and 200 mm (8 in) squares and 200 × 100 mm (8 × 4 in) rectangles; hexagons are also available in plain colours, and a popular variation is a plain octagonal tile which is laid with small square coloured or decorated inserts at the intersections.

TYPES OF WALL AND FLOOR TILES *(continued)*

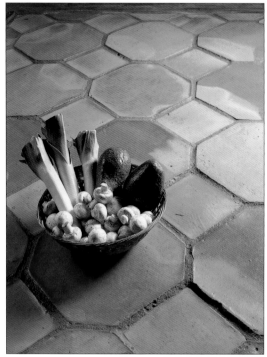

Quarry tiles are unglazed ceramic floor tiles with a brown, buff or reddish colour, and are a popular choice for hallways, conservatories and country-style kitchens. They are usually laid in a mortar bed, and after the joints have been grouted the tiles must be sealed with boiled linseed oil or a recommended proprietary sealer. Common sizes are 100 mm (4 in) and 150 mm (6 in) square. Special shaped tiles are also available for forming upstands at floor edges.

Terracotta tiles look similar to quarry tiles but are larger, and are fired at lower temperatures and so are more porous. They are sealed in the same way as quarry tiles. Squares, ranging in size between 200 and 400 mm (8 and 16 in), and rectangles are the commonest shapes, but octagons with small square infill tiles are also popular.

Mosaics

Mosaics are just tiny tiles – usually plain in colour, sometimes with a pattern –

Above: Handmade terracotta tiles exhibit a subtle variety of shade and colour, but need sealing to keep them clean.

Right: Ceramic tiles provide a durable and waterproof floor surface for bathrooms. Here dark blue square coloured corner inserts set off the dazzling white octagonal tiles.

Below: Mosaic tiles are once more regaining the popularity they enjoyed in times past, but laying them is definitely a labour of love.

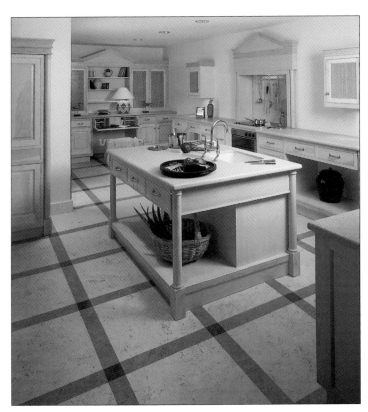

Modern lino tiles, made from natural materials rather than the plastic resins used in vinyl tiles, offer far better performance than traditional linoleum. They come in a range of bright and subtle colours and interesting patterns, often with pre-cut borders.

All these types generally come in 300 mm (12 in) squares, although larger squares and rectangles are available in some of the more expensive ranges. They are generally sold in packs of nine, covering roughly 1 sq yd (0.84 sq m), although many kinds are often available singly.

Above: Cork is the warmest of tiled floor coverings underfoot, and when sealed is good-looking and durable too.

Above: The more expensive types of vinyl floor tile offer superb imitations of other materials such as ceramic, wood, marble and terrazzo finishes.

which are sold made up in sheets on an open-weave cloth backing. These sheets are laid like larger tiles in a bed of adhesive, and all the gaps including those on the surface of the sheet are grouted afterwards. Square mosaics are the most common, but roundels, hexagons and other interlocking shapes are also available. Sheets are usually square and 300 mm (12 in) across, and are often sold in packs of five or ten. The best way of estimating quantities is to work out the area to be covered and to divide that by the coverage figure given on the pack to work out how many packs to buy. Note that wall and floor types are of different thicknesses, as with ordinary ceramic tiles.

Cork, vinyl and lino tiles

Cork tiles come in a small range of colours and textures. Their surface feels warm and relatively soft underfoot, and they also give some worthwhile heat and sound insulation – particularly useful in bathrooms, kitchens, halls and even children's bedrooms. The cheapest types have to be sealed to protect the surface after they have been laid, but the more expensive vinyl-coated floor types can be walked on as soon as they have been stuck down. They need little more than an occasional wash and polish to keep them in good condition. However, even the best cork floor tiles are prone to damage from sharp heels and heavy furniture, for example.

Vinyl tiles come in a very wide range of plain and patterned types, and generally resist wear better than cork, so they can be used on floors subject to fairly heavy wear. However, they are a little less gentle on the feet. Some of the more expensive types give very passable imitations of luxury floor coverings such as marble and terrazzo. Most are made in self-adhesive form and very little maintenance is needed once they have been laid.

TILING TOOLS AND EQUIPMENT

Tools for ceramic tiles

For almost any ceramic tiling job, large or small, the following are needed: tile adhesive; a notched adhesive spreader; some tile spacers; lengths of tile edge trim (optional); grout plus a flexible spreader; a steel tape measure; some lengths of 38 × 12 mm (1^1/$_2$ × ^{1}/$_2$ in) softwood battening (furring strips), plus masonry pins and a hammer for supporting the tiles on large wall areas; a spirit level; a tile cutter; a tile saw; a tile file; a piece of dowel for shaping the grout lines; a pencil and felt-tip pen; some sponges and cloths for wiping and polishing. Some silicone sealant or mastic (caulking) may also be needed for waterproofing joints where tiling abuts baths, basins and shower trays.

Tile cutters range from the basic – an angled cutting tip attached to a handle – to elaborate cutting jigs that guarantee perfectly accurate cuts every time. A tile saw is useful for making shaped cutouts to fit around obstacles such as pipework, and a tile file helps to smooth cut edges.

Both adhesive and grout for wall tiling are now usually sold ready-mixed in plastic tubs complete with a notched plastic spreader. For areas that will get the occasional splash or may suffer from condensation, a water-resistant adhesive and grout is perfectly adequate, but for surfaces such as shower cubicles which will have to withstand prolonged wetting it is essential to use both waterproof adhesive and waterproof grout. Always use waterproof grout on tiled worktops; ordinary grout will harbour germs.

Grout is generally white, but coloured grout is on sale and will make a feature of the grout lines (an effect that looks best with plain or fairly neutral patterned tiles).

TILING TOOLS, MATERIALS AND EQUIPMENT

These include a tile saw (**1**), adhesive (**2**), a polishing cloth (**3**), a spirit level (**4**), tile edge nippers (**5**), a tile cutter/snapper (**6**) or a tiling jig (**7**), a tile scriber (**8**), a tile cutter with width and angle jig (**9**), a heavy duty tile cutter (**10**), tile files (**11**) or a tile edge sander with abrasive strips (**12**), masking tape (**13**), masonry nails (**14**), a hammer (**15**), a homemade tile gauge (**16**), a retractable steel measure (**17**), a pencil (**18**), adhesive spreaders (**19** and **27**), a grout finisher (**20**) or dowel (**21**), tile edging trim (**22**), small and large tile spacers (**23**), a grout remover (**24**), a grout spreader (**25**), grout (**26**) and battens (furring strips) (**28**).

Ceramic floor tile adhesive is widely available in powder form as well as ready-mixed. It is best always to use a waterproof type (plus waterproof grout), even in theoretically dry areas.

Adhesive and grout are both sold in a range of sizes, sometimes labelled by weight, sometimes by volume; always check the coverage specified by the manufacturer on the packaging when buying, so as not to overbuy or run out halfway through the job.

Tools for cork, vinyl and lino tiles

Only a few simple tools are needed to lay cork and vinyl tiles, but, except for the self-adhesive type, special tile adhesive is required. This is sold ready-mixed in tubs, and usually comes complete with a notched spreader.

Special water-based adhesive is the type to choose for both cork and lino tiles; solvent-based contact adhesives were formerly the first choice, but their fumes are extremely unpleasant and also dangerously inflammable, and they are no longer recommended. For vinyl-coated cork tiles a special vinyl acrylic adhesive is needed. For vinyl tiles, an emulsion-type latex flooring adhesive is the best choice.

For unsealed cork tiles a sealer is required. Ordinary polyurethane varnish, as used for furniture, will do; there are also special floor sealers. Three coats will be needed.

Tools are simply a tape measure, a sharp utility knife and a steel straightedge for marking and cutting border tiles. A proprietary profile gauge with sliding steel or plastic needles makes it easy to cut tiles to fit round awkward obstacles such as architraves (trims) and pipework. But it is just as effective, and less costly, to cut a template from card or paper.

SETTING OUT TILED AREAS

The best way to practise tiling skills is to begin by covering just a small area such as a washbasin splashback, where setting out the tiles so that they are centred on the area concerned is a simple job and there is very little tile cutting to do.

For a larger area – a whole wall, or perhaps even a complete room – exactly the same techniques are used. The big difference is the sheer scale of the job, which makes the preliminary setting-out by far the most important part. The problem is that walls are seldom blank surfaces, and there may be a number of obstacles to tile around. Care must be taken to get the best fit around them with these inflexible tile squares, without needing to cut impossibly thin slivers to fill in gaps.

The most important thing to do is to plan precisely where the whole tiles will fall. On a flat, uninterrupted wall this is quite easy; simply find the centre line of the wall and plan the tiling to start from

there. However, there will probably be obstacles such as window reveals, door openings and built-in furniture in the room, all competing to be the centre of attention, and it will be necessary to work out the best 'centre point' while all the time trying to avoid having very thin cut tile borders and edges.

It is best to use a device called a *tiling gauge* – a batten (furring strip) marked out in tile widths – to work this out. The gauge is easy to make from a straight piece of timber about 1.2 m (4 ft) long, marked off with pencil lines to match the size of the tile. Use this to ensure that the tiles will be centred accurately on major features such as window reveals, with a border of cut tiles of equal width at the end of each row or column of tiles.

The next stage is the actual setting-out. With large areas of tiling, two things are vitally important. First, the tile rows must be exactly horizontal; if they are not, errors will accumulate as

the tiles extend across the wall, throwing the verticals out of alignment with disastrous results. When tiling right around a room, inaccurate levels mean that rows do not match up at the start and finish point. Second, the tiles need some support while the adhesive sets; without it, they may slump down the wall.

The solution is to fix a line of battens across the wall – or right around the room – just above the level of the skirting (baseboard), securing them with partly-driven masonry nails so that they can be removed later when the adhesive has set. The precise level will be dictated by setting-out with the tiling gauge, but will usually be between half and three-quarters of a tile width above the skirting. Do not rely on this being level; it may not be. Draw the line out in pencil first, using the spirit level, and then pin the battens up and check the level again. If everything is straight, it is time to start tiling.

TILING AROUND A DOOR

1 If the door is close to the room corner, start with whole tiles next to the frame. Use a vertical tile guide if the architrave (trim) is not truly vertical.

2 Tile the whole of the main wall area, adding cut tiles next to the room corner and at ceiling level. Remove the tile supports when the adhesive has set.

3 Fit a tile support above the door in line with the tile rows, and another between it and the other room corner, just above skirting (baseboard) level.

5 Here the panel is being surrounded by slim border tiles. Add whole tiles to the top of the panel first, working from the centre line outwards.

6 At the corners of the panel, fit an over-long horizontal tile and hold another vertically over it so you can mark a 45° cutting line on each tile.

7 Make the 45° cuts on the end of each corner tile, then bed the horizontal tile in place. Check that the cut end is precisely aligned with the panel corner.

8 Repeat the process at the other end of the horizontal section of the border. Both end pieces should be the same length, as the border is centred.

9 Fit the border tiles up each side of the decorative panel, then mark the position of the mitre cut on the last tiles, cut them and fit them in place.

Right: The finished panel, neatly centred as a decorative splashback above a washbasin.

USING MOSAICS AND CORK TILES

Small mosaic tiles are an attractive alternative to square or rectangular tiles, especially for small areas of tiling where their size will look particularly appropriate. Modern mosaic tiles come in a range of shapes and sizes, from simple squares and roundels to interlocking shapes such as hexagons. They are generally sold in sheets backed with an open-mesh cloth that holds the individual mosaic pieces at the correct spacing and greatly speeds up the installation process, since the entire sheet is stuck to the wall in one go. If cut pieces are needed to fill in the perimeter of the tiled area, simply cut individual mosaic tiles from the sheet with scissors, trim them to size with a tile cutter and position them one by one. Mosaic tiles are fixed and grouted with ordinary tiling products.

One other type of wall tile is popular as a wall covering. Cork tiles are made by compressing the bark of the cork tree into blocks, and then slicing them up into squares – 300 mm (12 in) is the commonest size – or rectangles. They come in a range of natural shades, and may also be stained or printed with surface designs during manufacture. They are stuck to the wall surface with a special water-based contact adhesive, and since they are virtually impossible to remove once placed, they should be regarded as a long-term decorative option and their use carefully planned beforehand.

TIP

If using cork tiles on walls, change the faceplate screws on light switches and socket outlets (receptacles) for longer ones; the originals will be too short to reach the lugs in the mounting box.

USING MOSAIC TILES

1 Start by putting up a horizontal tile support and a vertical tiling guide, as for ordinary tiling. Then apply an area of tile adhesive to the wall.

2 Position the first sheet of mosaic tiles on the wall, in the angle between the tiling support and the tiling guide, and press it firmly into place.

USING CORK TILES

1 To ensure that the tile rows and columns build up correctly, draw horizontal and vertical pencil guidelines on the wall. Place the first tile.

2 If border tiles are to be cut, hold a whole tile over the last whole tile fixed, butt another against the frame and mark its edge on the tile underneath it.

3 After positioning several sheets, use a mallet and a piece of plywood to tamp the mosaics down evenly. Use a towel or a thin carpet offcut as a cushion. Ensure the grouting spaces between each sheet are equal.

4 To fill in the perimeter of the area, snip individual mosaic tiles from the sheet, cut them to the size required and bed them in the adhesive.

5 Spread grout over the tiled area, working it well into the gaps between the individual mosaics. Wipe off excess grout, and polish the surface when dry.

3 Place the marked tile on a board and cut it with a sharp utility knife. The exposed part of the sandwiched tile in step 2 will fit the border gap precisely.

4 Fit the cut piece of border tile in place on the wall. Shave or sand its cut edge down a fraction if it is a tight fit. Cut and fit others in the same way.

5 To fit a tile around an obstacle such as a light switch, make a paper or card template and test its fit before cutting the actual tile.

6 Run a rolling pin or a length of broom handle over the completed surface to ensure that all the tiles are well bonded to the wall.

SETTING OUT TILED FLOORS

Like tiled walls, tiled floors need careful setting-out if the end result is to look neat and professional. This is especially important with glazed ceramic and quarry tiles and also patterned vinyl and lino tiles, but matters rather less with plain vinyl or cork tiles where the finished effect is of uniform colour and the joints between the tiles are practically invisible.

Fortunately the necessary setting-out is much easier with floor tiles than wall tiles, since the tiles can be dry-laid on the floor surface and moved around until a starting point is found that gives the best arrangement, with cut border tiles of approximately equal size all around the perimeter of the room.

In a regular-shaped room, start by finding the actual centre point of the floor, by linking the midpoints of opposite pairs of walls with string lines. In an irregularly-shaped room, place string lines as shown in the illustration so that they avoid obstructions, and then link the midpoints of opposite pairs of strings to find the room's centre. Now dry-lay rows of tiles out towards the walls in each direction, remembering to allow for the joint thickness if appropriate, to see how many whole tiles will fit in and to check whether this starting point results in over-narrow border tiles or awkward cuts against obstacles. Move the rows slightly to improve the fit if necessary, then chalk the string lines and snap them against the floor surface to mark the starting point.

Left: Quarry and terracotta tiles provide a durable and attractive floor covering and are especially suited to kitchens and conservatories. To ensure that the tiles are correctly aligned with equal borders around the perimeter of the room, it is essential to follow the correct setting-out procedures.

5 To cut border tiles, lay a whole tile over the last whole tile laid, butt another against the skirting (baseboard) and mark its edge on the tile underneath.

6 Place the marked tile on a board and cut it with a sharp utility knife. The exposed part of the sandwiched tile in step 5 will fit the border gap perfectly.

7 Fit the cut piece of border tile in place. Trim its edge slightly if it is a tight fit. Mark, cut and fit the other border tiles in exactly the same way.

8 To cut a tile at an external corner, lay a whole tile over the last whole tile in one adjacent row, butt another against the wall and draw along its edge.

9 Move the sandwiched tile to the other side of the corner, again butt the second whole tile against the wall and mark its edge on the sandwiched tile.

10 Use the utility knife to cut out the square waste section along the marked lines, and offer up the L-shaped border tile to check its fit before fixing it.

SEALING CORK TILES

When laying unsealed cork tiles, take care not to get adhesive on the faces of the tiles, and seal the surface with three coats of polyurethane varnish or a proprietary cork sealer to protect the surface from dirt and moisture. If access to the room is necessary while the floor is being sealed, do half the floor one day and the other half the next day.

LAYING FLOOR COVERINGS

The wide range of floor coverings includes carpets, sheet vinyl, and decorative wood panels and strips.

Carpets laid loose have been used on floors for millennia, but it is only a few decades ago that wall-to-wall fitted carpeting became widely popular. Traditional woven carpets made from natural fibres have been challenged by carpets made from synthetic fibres and by alternative methods of manufacture. There is now a huge choice of colours and patterns in types to suit all locations and wear conditions, available in various widths.

Sheet vinyl floor coverings come in a huge range of colours and patterns, and may also have a surface embossed along the lines of the design to give plausible imitations of other floor coverings such as tiles, marble, wood and cork. Some more expensive types have a cushioned underside formed by incorporating small air bubbles during manufacture, which makes them warmer and softer underfoot than their solid counterparts.

There are two main types of wooden floor covering, wood-block, sometimes called wood mosaic, and wood-strip. The former consists of small slivers of wood (usually a hardwood) laid in groups and stuck to strong cloth to form wooden 'tiles', while the latter is just what its name implies: narrow hardwood planks laid over an existing floor.

Opposite: Fitted carpet is still the most popular choice for living rooms, and the combination of hardwearing fibres and stunning designs now available makes it possible to complement and enhance any style of interior.

TYPES OF FLOOR COVERING

When choosing new floor coverings, remember that there is more to it than simply ordering wall-to-wall carpet throughout, and mistakes can be expensive. Floor coverings have to withstand a great deal of wear and tear in certain areas of the average home, especially if there are children or animals in the family, so choosing what to put where is very important.

There is a wide choice of materials on the market, and laying them is well within the capability of most people. Shopping for floor coverings has never been easier either. All the major do-it-yourself suppliers stock a huge range of materials – plus all the tools and accessories needed to lay them. If they do not stock exactly what is required, there are also specialist flooring and carpet suppliers.

Carpets

Carpets consist of fibre tufts or loops woven or stuck to a durable backing. *Woven* carpets are generally the most expensive. Modern types are made by either the Axminster or the Wilton method, which differ in technical details but both produce a durable product which can be patterned or plain. *Tufted* carpets are made by stitching tufts of fibre into a woven backing, where they are secured by attaching a second backing under the first with adhesive. Some of the less expensive types have a foam underlay bonded directly to the backing; others require a separate underlay.

A wide range of fibre types is used in carpet construction today, including wool, nylon, acrylic, polypropylene and viscose rayon. Fibre blends can improve carpet performance; a mixture of 80 per cent wool and 20 per cent nylon is particularly popular for providing a combination of warmth, resilience, wear, low flammability and resistance to soiling.

Pile length and density affect the carpet's performance as well as its looks, and most carpets are classified to indicate the sort of wear they can be expected to withstand. The pile can be *cut*, often to different lengths, giving a sculptured effect; *looped* (shag), that is, uncut and left long; *corded*, which means uncut and pulled tight to the backing; or *twisted*, which gives a tufty effect. A dense pile wears better than a loosely woven one which can be parted to reveal the backing.

Carpet widths are described as *broadloom*, more than 1.8 m (6 ft) wide; or *body* (stair carpet), usually up to 900 mm (3 ft) wide. The former are intended for large areas, the latter for corridors and stairs. Broadloom carpet is available in various imperial and metric widths.

Carpet tiles

These are small squares of carpet of various types, designed to be loose-laid.

Cheaper tiles resemble cord and felt carpets, while more expensive ones may have a short or long cut pile. Common sizes are 300, 450, 500 and 600 mm (12, 18, 20 and 24 in) square.

Sheet vinyl flooring

This is a relatively thin material which provides a smooth, hygienic and easy-to-clean floor covering that is widely used in rooms such as kitchens, bathrooms and hallways. It is made from layers of plastic resins, with a clear wear layer protecting the printed design and frequently with an air cushion layer between this and the backing for extra comfort and warmth underfoot. It is fairly flexible and easy to cut for an exact fit; it is generally loose-laid, with double-sided adhesive tape used only at seams and edges.

Sheet linoleum (lino) is also becoming popular again for domestic use, and is available in some stylish designs and colourways with optional contrasting border designs. Lino is more difficult for the amateur to lay,

TYPES OF FLOOR COVERING (*continued*)

however, being heavier, less flexible and harder to cut than sheet vinyl.

Vinyl flooring is available in a wide range of designs, including realistic imitations of ceramic tiles, wood, cork and stone. It is sold by the linear metre (or yard) from rolls 2, 3 or 4 m (6 ft 6 in, 10 ft or 13 ft) wide; the larger width enables seamfree floors to be laid in most medium-sized rooms.

Above: Modern sheet linoleum has taken on a new lease of life, offering a range of sophisticated colourways teamed with stylish borders that are perfect for kitchens, utility rooms and hallways.

Left: Sealed cork flooring offers a unique combination of warmth and resilience underfoot, coupled with an easy-clean surface that looks attractive too.

Below: Solid wood-strip flooring, shown here in beech, provides a luxury floor covering that looks stunning and will also last a lifetime.

Wood floor coverings

These come in two main forms: as square wood-block panels made up of individual fingers of wood stuck to a cloth or felt backing for ease of handling and laying; or as wood-strip flooring – interlocking planks, often of veneer on a plywood backing. They are laid over the existing floor surface; most are tongued-and-grooved, so only occasional nailing or clipping is required to hold them in place.

Wood-block panels are usually 300 or 450 mm (12 or 18 in) square, while planks are generally 75 or 100 mm (3 or 4 in) wide and come in a range of lengths to allow the end joints to be staggered from one row to the next.

Left: Wood is an excellent choice for entrance halls too, where a durable yet good-looking floor surface is essential.

are extremely hardwearing kitchen carpets available, with a specially treated short nylon pile that is easy to keep clean, and also water-resistant bathroom carpets that give a touch of luxury underfoot without turning into a swamp at bathtime.

Leisure areas – living rooms, dining rooms and bedrooms – are commonly carpeted wall to wall. Do not be tempted to skimp on quality in living rooms, which get the most wear and tend to develop distinct traffic routes. However, it is reasonable to choose light-duty types for bedrooms.

Alternatives to carpets depend simply on taste in home decor. Options include sanded and sealed floorboards teamed with scatter rugs, or a parquet perimeter to a fine specimen carpet. Sheet vinyl or cork tiles may also be worth considering for children's rooms.

Room-by-room choices

In principle it is possible to lay any floor covering in any room of a home. However, custom and the practicalities of life tend to divide the home into three broad areas.

Access areas such as halls, landings and stairs need a floor covering that is able to cope with heavy traffic and muddy shoes. Ideal choices for hallways are materials with a water-repellent and easy-clean surface – for example, sheet vinyl, vinyl tiles, a wood-strip or wood-block floor, sanded and sealed floorboards, or glazed ceramic or quarry tiles. For stairs, where safety is paramount, the best material to choose is a heavy-duty carpet with a short pile, which can also be used on landings.

Work areas such as kitchens and bathrooms also need durable floor coverings that are easy to clean and, especially in the case of bathrooms, water-resistant as well. Sheet vinyl is a popular choice for both rooms, but tiles of various types can also provide an excellent surface – sealed cork, with its warm feel underfoot, is particularly suitable in bathrooms. However, if carpet is preferred for these rooms there

Below: Sanded floorboards can be further enhanced with a delicate stencilled border design. Always seal floorboards with several coats of good quality varnish for a hard-wearing finish.

FLOORING TOOLS AND EQUIPMENT

For laying *carpet* the basic essentials are a tape measure and a sharp utility knife with a good supply of extra blades for cutting and trimming the carpet to fit. As an alternative, special carpet shears can be used.

For a *woven carpet* a carpet stretcher is invaluable. This is a device with a horizontal pad of metal spikes at one end which is locked into the carpet, and a cushioned pad at the other end which is nudged with the knee to stretch the carpet into place. It is probably best to hire this relatively expensive tool, which will not be needed very often.

Also needed are some carpet gripper strips to hold the carpet in position around the perimeter of the room. Gripper strips are thin strips of plywood fitted with angled nails that grip the underside of the carpet, and they are themselves nailed to the floor about 10 mm (³/₈ in) from the skirting (baseboard) all around the room. The edge of the carpet is then tucked down into the gap, usually with a carpet fitter's bolster. A wide brick bolster (stonecutter's) chisel may be used instead, as long as it is clean.

A range of tools for laying carpet, vinyl and wooden floorings include: gripper rods (**1**), a single-sided brass threshold (saddle) strip (**2**), an aluminium carpet-to-vinyl strip (**3**), a threshold cover strip (**4**), a carpet-to-carpet strip (**5**), right-handed (**6**) or left-handed (**7**) carpet shears, a carpet knife with spare blades (**8**), staples (**9**) and a staple hammer (**10**), a recess scriber (**11**), a tack hammer (**12**), a carpet fitter's bolster (**13**), dividers (**14**), an adjustable straightedge (**15**), hessian (burlap) carpet tape (**16**), liquid adhesive (**17**), double-sided tape (**18**), a retractable steel tape measure (**19**), a carpet stretcher (**20**), a tenon saw (**21**), a pad saw (**22**), a coping saw (**23**) and an electric jigsaw (saber saw) (**24**).

Foam-backed carpet does not need gripper strips. It may be stapled to the floor with a staple gun, or stuck down with double-sided adhesive tape. For both woven and foam-backed types, adhesive seaming tape may also be needed to join sections of carpet together and threshold (saddle) strips to neatly finish the carpeted edge off at door openings.

For laying *sheet vinyl*, again a tape measure and a sharp utility knife are needed. A long steel straightedge will also be invaluable. For bonding the lengths to the floor along edges and seams, use either double-sided tape or bands of liquid adhesive, spread with a toothed spreader. Lastly, a pair of compasses or a scribing block and pencil, plus a shape tracer, are needed to transfer onto the sheet the outlines of the various floor-level obstacles around the edge of the room.

For laying *wood-block* and *wood-strip* floor coverings, the requirements are general woodworking tools, some adhesive and a spreader for wood-block floors, and pins (tacks) or fixing clips for wood-strip floors, plus varnish or sealer if laying an unsealed type.

UNDERLAYS

Lining paper or cloth underlay is recommended for foam-backed carpets as it prevents the foam from sticking to the floor surface. For woven carpets use either a foam or felt underlay: they are available in various grades and should be matched to the carpet being laid. Heavy-duty underlays are recommended for heavy wear areas such as hallways, or where extra insulation is required.

PREPARING WOOD FLOORS

Securing loose boards

For suspended wood floors – boards laid over floor joists – start by lifting the old floor covering and checking that all the boards are securely fixed to their joists, and that they are reasonably flat and level. Loose boards will creak annoyingly when walked on, and raised edges or pronounced warping may show as lines through the new floor covering.

Use either cut nails or large oval-headed nails to secure loose boards. When driving them near known pipe or cable runs, take care not to pierce them; it is best to drive the new nails as close to existing nail positions as possible for safety.

Laying hardboard

Covering the existing boards with a hardboard underlay is an alternative to floor sanding as a way of ensuring a smooth, flat surface ideal for thin sheet floor coverings. Lay the boards in rows with the joints staggered from row to row, and pin them down with hardboard pins driven in at 150 mm

(6 in) spacings. Lay separate strips above known pipe runs.

If preparing to lay glazed ceramic or quarry tiles on a suspended wood floor, put down exterior-grade plywood.

Sanding floors

Where old floorboards are very uneven, or it is planned to leave them exposed but they are badly stained and marked, hire a floor sanding machine. This resembles a cylinder (reel) lawnmower, with a drum to which sheets of abrasive paper are fitted. A bag at the rear collects the sawdust; however, always wear a face mask when sanding floors. Also hire a smaller disc or belt sander for finishing off the room edges.

If necessary, drive any visible nail heads below the surface. Start sanding with coarse abrasive paper, running the machine at 45° to the board direction, then use medium and fine paper in turn with the machine running parallel to the boards. Use the disc or belt sander to tackle the perimeter of the room where the large sander cannot reach.

SECURING FLOORBOARDS

1 Drive in any nails that have lifted due to warping or twisting of the floorboards, and then recess their heads slightly using a nail punch.

2 If nails will not hold the floorboard flat against the joist, drill pilot and clearance holes and use wood screws to secure the board firmly in place.

TIP

When sanding floorboards, always raise the drum at the end of each pass to prevent the abrasives from damaging the boards while the machine is stationary.

LAYING HARDBOARD

1 If hardboard sheets are used as an underlay for a new floor covering, start by punching in any raised nail heads all over the floor.

2 Nail the hardboard sheets to the floorboards at 150 mm (6 in) intervals along the edges and also 300 mm (12 in) apart across the face of each sheet.

SANDING FLOORBOARDS

1 Use a floor sander to smooth and strip old floorboards. Drape the flex (cord) over one shoulder and raise the drum before starting the machine up.

2 Run the machine at 45° to the board direction to start with, first in one direction and then in the other at right angles to the original passes.

3 Then switch to a medium-grade abrasive and run the sander back and forth parallel with the board direction. Finish off with fine-grade abrasive.

4 Use a smaller disc or belt sander to strip areas close to the skirtings (baseboards) and door thresholds, where the larger drum sander cannot reach.

5 Use a scraper to remove paint or varnish from inaccessible areas such as around pipework, then sand the stripped wood smooth by hand.

PREPARING SOLID FLOORS

Ground floors of solid concrete are prone to two main problems: cracking or potholing of the surface, and rising damp caused by a failure in the damp-proof membrane within the floor structure. Cracks and depressions may show through new floor coverings, especially thinner types such as sheet vinyl, while dampness will encourage mould growth beneath the covering.

Relatively narrow cracks can be patched with a repair mortar of 1 part cement to 3 parts sand, or an exterior-quality masonry filler.

If the floor surface is uneven or pitted, it can be covered with a thin layer of self-smoothing compound. There are two types available; both are powders and are mixed with either water or with a special latex emulsion. The mixture is made up in a bucket and poured onto the floor surface, trowelling it out to a thickness of about 3 mm ($1/8$ in). The liquid finds its own level and dries to give a hard, smooth surface which can be walked on in about 1 hour. Leave it to dry for 24 hours before laying a floor covering over it.

An alternative approach is to cover the concrete with a floating floor of chipboard (particle board), if raising the floor level will not cause problems at door thresholds. The boards can be laid directly on the concrete over heavy-duty polythene (polyethylene) sheeting, which acts as a vapour barrier. If additional insulation is required, put down polystyrene boards first and then lay the new flooring over them.

Treat damp floors immediately with one or two coats of a proprietary damp-proofing liquid.

LAYING A SELF-SMOOTHING COMPOUND

1 Start by sweeping the floor clear of dust and debris. Then scrub away any patches of grease from the surface with strong detergent solution.

2 Key the surface of vinyl floor tiles by sanding it before laying the compound. Wipe away the dust with a damp cloth.

3 If the concrete surface is very dusty or appears unduly porous, seal it by brushing on a generous coat of diluted PVA adhesive (white general-purpose adhesive).

4 Mix up the self-smoothing compound in a bucket, following the manufacturer's instructions carefully to ensure that the mix is the right consistency and free from lumps.

5 Starting in the corner farthest from the room door, pour the compound out onto the floor surface to cover an area of about 1 sq m (11 sq ft).

6 Use a plasterer's trowel to smooth the compound out to a thickness of about 3 mm ($1/8$ in). Mix, pour and level further batches as required.

LAYING A CHIPBOARD FLOOR

1 You can level and insulate a concrete floor by laying a floating floor of chipboard (particle board) over it. Put down heavy-duty polythene (polyethylene) sheets first.

2 Tape the sheet to the walls; it will be hidden behind the new skirting (baseboard) later. Then butt-joint 25 mm (1 in) polystyrene insulation boards.

3 Cover the insulation with tongued-and-grooved flooring-grade boards. Use cut pieces as necessary, and add a tapered threshold (saddle) strip at the door.

REMOVING OLD FLOOR COVERINGS

Generally speaking, old floor coverings should always be lifted before laying new ones. This also provides an opportunity to inspect the floor itself and to carry out any repairs that may be necessary. However, there are some situations where it may not be practical or necessary to lift an existing floor covering – for example, where vinyl tiles have been laid over a concrete floor and they are firmly stuck to it. Stripping such a large area will be an extremely time-consuming job unless a professional floor tile stripping machine is hired.

1 The backing of old foam-backed carpets may remain stuck to the floor surface. Brush it up, and also remove any remaining staples or seaming tape.

2 To lift vinyl tiles or sheet vinyl that has been stuck along edges and seams, use a heat gun to soften the adhesive and quickly pull up the flooring.

3 If vinyl or cork tiles have been stuck onto a hardboard underlay, lift a few tiles to expose the board edges and then lever the boards up in one piece.

4 Lift wood-block or wood-strip floors if they are damaged or show signs of lifting. Otherwise cover them by pinning on a hardboard overlay.

PAINTING AND VARNISHING FLOORS

Rather than being replaced, floors can simply be brightened up with paint or varnish. This is not only economical, but can create some effects that an off-the-shelf material cannot provide. This technique can be used directly on both solid and wooden floors as long as the surface is in good condition. If it is not, cover floorboards with a hardboard overlay, or treat solid floors with a self-smoothing compound.

Concrete floors can be given a smooth, washable and durable finish by using special floor paint. Make sure the surface is clean, dry and free from oil or grease. Then apply the first coat thinned with white spirit (paint thinner) to act as a sealer, and add two further full-strength coats.

Varnishing bare floorboards, especially after they have been stripped with a floor sander, can create a stunning floor that will contrast beautifully with loose-laid rugs. A stain can be applied before the varnish if wanted. Simply prepare the floor in the same way as any other indoor woodwork, repairing any major surface defects and checking that nail heads are well punched down. If using stain, apply sparingly with a cloth along the grain direction and leave it to dry. Apply three coats of clear varnish to seal the surface. Alternatively, use a coloured sealer to do both jobs with one product. Paint can also be used if it is preferred to hide the grain of the wood.

Stencils or other patterns can be applied either direct to the boards or to a hardboard overlay. A tiled effect can be created by putting down hardboard squares that have been decorated with a special paint effect such as marbling. At least three coats of varnish should be applied over any painted effect, or it will soon wear away.

PAINTING CONCRETE FLOORS
Seal and decorate concrete floors in areas such as utility rooms by applying a proprietary floor paint with a paint roller on an extension pole.

STAIN EFFECTS
Stain and varnish new or stripped floorboards after sanding them smooth and filling any defects. Use a cardboard mask if applying more than one shade.

STENCIL DESIGNS
Effects such as stencils can be applied to a stained or painted floor. Mark out the line of the pattern on the floor and stencil on the design.

1 **PAINTING HARDBOARD** Cover poor-quality floorboards with hardboard, laid with the smooth side uppermost, then paint on the chosen design. Use a strip of wood as a guide.

2 Alternatively, use masking tape to outline the design, apply the paint, and remove the tape when the paint is just touch-dry.

3 With any painted effect, allow the paint to dry hard, then seal the floor surface with three coats of clear varnish or floor sealer.

Above: Here plain floorboards have been enhanced with a two-colour painted diamond design, an effect that tones well with the simple painted decor.

LAYING FOAM-BACKED CARPET

Laying traditional woven carpet can be difficult for the amateur, because it has to be correctly tensioned across the room by using gripper strips and a carpet stretcher if it is to wear well. Because of the cost of such carpet, it may be considered best to leave the job to professionals. However, there is no reason why the do-it-yourselfer should not get some practice by laying less expensive foam-backed carpet in, for example, a spare bedroom. It is possible to disguise any slight inaccuracies that creep into the cutting and fitting process more easily here than with smooth sheet floor coverings such as vinyl, so the job is a good introduction to the general technique of laying roll floor coverings.

Start by putting down a paper or cloth underlay on the floor, taping the joins and stapling the underlay down so that it cannot creep as work continues. Unroll the carpet across the room, with the excess lapping up the walls. Roughly trim the excess all around the room, leaving 50 mm (2 in) for final trimming. Make small cuts at external corners such as around chimney breasts (fireplace projections), and let the tongues fall back into alcoves, then trim off the waste across the face of the chimney breast. Next, press the carpet into internal corners and mark the corner point with a finger. Make cuts to remove the triangle of carpet from the internal angle. Finally, trim the perimeter with a knife drawn along the angle between skirting (baseboard) and wall, and secure the edges with double-sided adhesive tape. Fit a threshold (saddle) strip across door openings.

1 Before laying a foam-backed carpet, put down a paper or cloth underlay to keep the foam from sticking to the floor. Tape joins and staple it in place.

2 Put double-sided adhesive tape all around the perimeter of the room, then unroll the carpet and position it so that it laps up the room walls.

3 Butt the edge of the carpet up against the longest straight wall in the room. Peel the backing paper off the tape and bed the edge into place.

4 Work the carpet across the floor to the opposite wall to ensure that it is lying flat. Then trim that edge against the skirting (baseboard) and tape it down too.

5 Start fitting the carpet at the top of the flight, trimming each tread and riser in turn and then forcing a fold of carpet into the angled gripper strips.

6 On an open-string staircase, either trim the carpet to fit around each baluster or fold over the edge and tack it to fit against the baluster as shown here.

ALTERNATIVE FIXINGS

1 When fitting a stair runner rather than a full-width carpet, paint or stain the stair treads and anchor the carpet with stair rods.

7 On winder (curved) stairs, cut a piece of carpet to cover each tread and the riser beneath it. Align it so that the weave is at right angles to the riser.

8 Secure each piece of carpet to the gripper strip at the rear of the tread first, then stretch it over the tread and down to the next gripper strip.

2 If you are using foam-backed carpet on your stairs, fit special gripper strips for foam-backed carpet into the angles between treads and risers.

9 Trim off the waste from the bottom edge of the riser, then repeat the cutting and fitting sequence for any other winder steps on the flight.

10 If the flight finishes with a projecting bullnose step, trim and tack the carpet to the riser as shown and cover the riser with a separate strip.

LAYING SHEET VINYL

Sheet vinyl flooring can be difficult to lay because it is wide and comparatively stiff to handle, and edge cutting must be done accurately if gaps are not to be noticeable against skirtings (baseboards). Lengths of quadrant beading (a base shoe) can be pinned (tacked) around the perimeter of the room to disguise any serious mistakes.

Most rooms contain at least one long straight wall, and it is often easiest to butt one edge of the vinyl up against this first of all. Use a block of wood and a pencil to scribe the wall profile onto the vinyl and cut along this line for a perfect fit. Alternatively, simply press the vinyl into the angle between wall and floor and cut along it with the knife held at a 45° angle. Then press the ends of the length neatly against the walls at right angles to the first wall, make small diagonal cuts at internal and external angles, and trim the edges to fit there. Finally stick down the edges and any seams with double-sided adhesive tape. Finish off doorways with proprietary threshold (saddle) strips.

1 Unless the wall is perfectly straight, make a cut at the corner and trim the adjacent edges of the sheet with a sharp knife along the angle of wall and floor.

3 Use a similar technique for trimming the sheet around larger obstacles such as washbasin pedestals.

2 At door architraves (trims), make cuts into the edge of the sheet down to floor level so the sheet will lie flat, and trim off the tongues.

4 To join sheet vinyl edge to edge, overlap the two sheets so that the pattern matches and cut through both layers against a steel straightedge. Discard the waste strips.

5 Place a strip of double-sided tape underneath the joint line, peel off the backing paper and press the two cut edges firmly down onto the tape.

6 To fit the sheet around plumbing pipework, make a cut into it at the pipe position and then trim out a circle of the material to fit around it.

7 At door openings, fit a threshold (saddle) strip to anchor the edge of the sheet. Here an existing strip has been prised up and is being hammered down again.

Below: Sheet vinyl flooring is ideal for kitchens with its easy-to-clean surface. The cushioned types also offer extra warmth and softness underfoot.

MAKING TEMPLATES FOR SHEET VINYL

Where sheet vinyl flooring is being laid around unusually shaped obstacles such as washbasin pedestals and piping, the best way of getting an accurate fit is to make a template of the obstacle so that its shape can be transferred onto the vinyl. Use taped-together sheets of paper cut to roughly the outline of the room and the obstacle. Tape the template to the floor, and use a block of wood and a pencil (or a pair of compasses) to draw a line on the template parallel with the outline of the obstacle.

Next, transfer the template to the vinyl, and use the same block of wood or compass setting to scribe lines back onto the vinyl itself. These lines will accurately represent the shape of the room and the obstacle. Cut along them and remove the waste, then stick down edges and seams as before.

1 Use a block and pencil to scribe the wall outline onto the paper.

2 Tape the template over the sheet vinyl and use the same block with a pencil to scribe a copy of the room outline back onto the vinyl.

PREPARING THE TEMPLATE

To make a cutting template for a room full of obstacles, such as a bathroom, tape sheets of paper together with their edges about 50 mm (2 in) from the room walls all around. Tear in from the edges to fit the template around the obstacles as shown, ready for the outline of the room and the obstacles to be scribed onto the template.

3 Use the same scribing technique as in step 1 to draw the outline of obstacles such as washbasin pedestals onto the paper template.

4 Repeat step 2 to scribe the outline of the obstacle onto the vinyl. Fix the pencil to the block with tape or a rubber band if that makes it easier to use.

5 Using a sharp utility knife, cut carefully around the outline of the obstacle. Make a cut into the waste area, test the cutout for fit, and trim it slightly if necessary.

6 To make cutouts around pipes, use a slim block and a pencil to scribe the pipe position onto the template as four lines at right angles to each other.

7 Place the template over the vinyl at the pipe position, and use the same block and pencil to mark the cutout on the vinyl as a small square.

8 Use compasses or a pipe offcut to draw a circle inside the square, then cut carefully round the circle and cut into the waste area from the edge.

LAYING WOOD MOSAIC FLOORING

The least expensive way of getting a decorative timber floor finish is by laying mosaic floor tiles, which are square tiles made up from a number of small fingers of decorative hardwood mounted on a cloth or felt backing sheet. This acts as an underlay as well as bonding the fingers together; the result is a sheet that will bend along the joint lines, and so can be easily cut to size if required. Alternatively, the fingers may be wired or stuck together to produce a rigid tile. In either case, tiles are generally either 300 mm (12 in) or 450 mm (18 in) square.

The fingers themselves may be solid wood or veneer on a cheaper softwood backing, and are usually arranged in a basketweave pattern; however, other patterns are also available. A wide range of wood types is used, including mahogany, teak, oak, iroko and merbau. Some tiles are supplied sealed, while others have to be varnished or sealed after being laid.

Laying wood-block floor tiles is a comparatively straightforward job, similar to any other floor tiling project in terms of preparation and setting-out. Store the panels unpacked in the room where they will be laid for at least seven days, to allow them to acclimatize to indoor temperature and humidity levels. This will help to reduce shrinkage or expansion after the tiles are laid. However, an expansion gap should always be left around the perimeter of the room.

1 Find the starting point in the same way as for other kinds of tile. Mark tiling guidelines on the floor and spread some adhesive in the first quarter.

2 Align the first tile carefully with the tiling guidelines and press it firmly down into the adhesive. Bed it down with a hammer and a wood offcut.

3 Lay the next panel in the same way, butting it up against its neighbour. Wipe off any adhesive from the tile faces immediately.

Left: Open fires, whether real or gas-powered, need a fire surround to frame them. Softwood mouldings with marble inserts look particularly effective.

Below: Even the simplest colour schemes gain a three-dimensional element from the use of wall panelling and mouldings.

the edges of roofs, but were soon also used inside on the perimeter of ceilings. As with panel mouldings, a huge range of profiles is available, from authentic Greek and Roman forms through eighteenth-and nineteenth-century styles, and featuring such classic motifs as acanthus, dentil, swag-and-drop and egg-and-dart. Wall and ceiling projections range from a delicate 32 mm (1^1/4 in) for single ogee (or cyma) types up to the massive 400 × 100 mm (16 × 4 in) of an ornate Adam-style frieze. Cornices are made in standard lengths, usually 2 or 3 metres or yards. Corners are formed by cutting mitres with a tenon or fine-toothed panel saw.

Plain concave mouldings – known as coving – are also available, made either as a paper-faced moulding with a plaster core, or machined from wood.

Ceiling roses

A ceiling rose is the perfect complement to a room with a cornice (crown molding) or ceiling panelling. It is a circular or elliptical moulding which can be used with or without a pendant light at its centre. A wide range of patterns is available, from classic designs to plainer modern versions. Sizes start at around 300 mm (12 in) in diameter and range up to a massive 1.5 × 1.2 m (5 × 4 ft) for the largest decorative ovals.

Wooden mouldings

The term 'moulding' is really a misnomer, better applied to decorative plasterwork which is, literally, moulded into shape. Timber mouldings are machined with shaped cutters and routers, to produce a wide range of cross sections.

Most everyday mouldings are machined either from softwood or from

Left: In high-ceilinged rooms, deeper skirtings (baseboards) and cornices (crown moldings) can help to make the ceiling appear lower. They can be picked out with contrasting shades of paint or matched to the wall colour.

WHAT TO ADD TO A ROOM (*continued*)

a cheap hardwood. As a general guideline, the larger mouldings – architraves (door and window trims), skirtings (baseboards) and the like – are cut from softwood, while mouldings with smaller and more intricate profiles are made from hardwood. Mouldings can be given a coloured finish, or other woods can be imitated, by staining and varnishing them.

Skirtings (baseboards)

These boards are fitted to plastered walls at ground level to protect the plaster surface from damage by careless feet or furniture – and incidentally to allow floor cleaning implements to be used right up to the floor edge without wetting or marking the walls. Until recently, the fashion was for fairly low, plain skirtings with either a pencil-

Below: Panelled doors can be made part of an overall colour scheme by highlighting the panel surrounds to match the other decorative mouldings in the room and to complement furnishing fabrics.

rounded or splayed-and-rounded cross section; these were usually painted. However, in many new homes there is now a switch back to deeper, more ornate skirtings with traditional profiles, often stained and varnished.

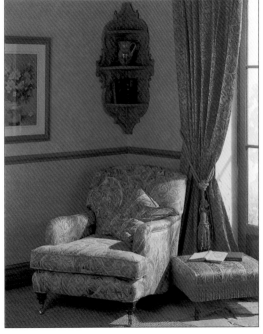

Left: Dado (chair) rails allow the use of different but complementary wall coverings above and below the rail. Picture-frame mouldings in a similar style and finish integrate the decorating scheme.

Architraves (trims)

These perform a similar job to skirtings (baseboards), being fitted around flush door and window openings to create a decorative and protective border. They are available in styles to match both plain and ornate skirtings, and are either run down to floor level, with the skirting abutting their outer edges, or rest on a small floor-level plinth block.

Dado (chair) and picture rails

These are horizontal mouldings fixed to wall surfaces, the former about 900 mm (3 ft) from the floor and the latter a short way below ceiling level. They were both popular until the 1930s, and are now making a comeback.

The dado rail was designed to protect the plaster from damage by the backs of chairs, and also provided a natural break in the wall's colour scheme. Traditionally the area below the rail – the whole surface was known as the dado (wainscot) – was panelled or finished in a relief wall covering, while that above it was papered or painted.

The picture rail allowed pictures to be hung – and moved about – at will, and also provided a visual break in rooms with high ceilings.

FITTING A NICHE

1 To fit an ornamental niche, spread a generous bed of adhesive all around the perimeter of the flat back, and add one or two blobs in the centre.

2 Press the niche into place on the wall, checking that it is truly vertical with a spirit level. Provide some temporary support if necessary.

3 Use a damp sponge to remove any adhesive that has been squeezed out around the perimeter of the niche. Do not disturb the niche while doing this.

Above Right: The niche installed, with its clever proportions making the recess appear deeper than it really is. Leave the adhesive to harden completely before putting anything on display.

CEILING ROSES

To add a ceiling rose, mark its position carefully, then apply adhesive to its rear face and press it into place. Wipe off excess adhesive. Heavy plaster types should be screwed to ceiling joists for security and the screw holes filled.

REPLACING TRIM MOULDINGS

Trim mouldings are both practical and decorative. They are used as skirtings (baseboards) to protect wall surfaces at floor level from accidental damage, and around door and window openings as architraves (trims) which frame the opening and disguise the joint between the frame and the wall surface. Both can be plain or ornate, and can be painted, stained or varnished. They may need replacing if they are damaged or simply look unfashionable.

Skirtings are often fixed directly to masonry walls with large cut nails in older homes, or with masonry nails in more recent ones. Alternatively, they may be nailed to rough timber fixing blocks or grounds (furrings) which are themselves nailed to the masonry. Boards fixed to blocks are much easier to remove than those nailed direct to the wall, since both cut and masonry nails can have a ferocious grip. In the latter situation it is often easier to punch the nails through the boards and into the walls than to try to prise them out. Boards on wood-framed walls are simply nailed to the frame, and so are easy to remove.

Architraves are pinned (tacked) in place to the edges of the door or window frame. It is an easy job to prise the trims away with a bolster (stonecutter's) chisel without causing undue damage to the frame or the surrounding wall surface.

REPLACING SKIRTINGS

1 To replace a small area of damaged skirting (baseboard), prise it away from the wall slightly, wedge it and use a tenon saw and mitre box to cut out a section.

2 Nail small support blocks behind the cut ends of the board, using masonry nails on solid walls, and then nail the cut ends to the support blocks.

3 Cut a piece of replacement board to fit, with its ends mitred to match the cutout section. Use plain wood if the skirting profile cannot be matched.

4 Nail the replacement board to the support blocks. If using plain wood, pin (tack) on decorative mouldings to build up a close match to the existing board.

5 When replacing whole lengths, use mitre joints at external corners. Fix the first length, then mark the inside of the mitre on the back of the next board.

6 Cut the mitre joints with a power saw with an adjustable sole plate. Set the cutting angle to just under 45° to ensure that the joint will fit well.

7 At internal corners, fit the first length right into the corner. Then scribe its profile onto the second board; cut this with a coping saw, and fit it.

REPLACING ARCHITRAVES

1 Prise off the old mouldings. They should come away easily. If necessary, lever against a block to avoid damaging the surface of the wall.

2 Hold an upright against the frame so that the inside of the mitre joint can be marked on it. Repeat for the other upright.

3 Cut the end of the moulding, using a mitre block or box. Alternatively, mark the line across the moulding with a protractor or combination square.

4 Fix the uprights to the frame by driving in nails at 300 mm (12 in) intervals. Recess the heads with a nail punch and fill the holes later.

5 Hold the top piece above the two uprights to mark the position for the mitre cut at each end. Make the cuts as before and test the piece for fit.

6 Nail the top piece to the frame, checking that the mitre joints are accurately aligned. Then drive a nail through each corner to secure the joint.

CREATING FIRE SURROUNDS

For those who are bored with the minimalist look of a simple hole-in-the-wall fireplace, a traditional fire surround and mantelshelf is just the thing. Complete fire surrounds are made in various types of wood or stone (and sometimes in a combination of the two), but they are relatively expensive and may not be precisely what is wanted. But it is possible to create the ideal effect, and save money into the bargain, by creating a custom-built surround from off-the-shelf planed timber (dressed lumber) and a range of decorative mouldings.

This simple design illustrates the basic principles of creating a tailor-made surround. Start by deciding on the overall height and width, and mark this on the wall around the fireplace opening. Then screw a series of vertical and horizontal support strips to the wall to act as fixing grounds for the various components of the surround.

The surround shown here is made from wood measuring 150 × 25 mm (6 × 1 in) and 50 × 25 mm (2 × 1 in). The mantelshelf and the crosspiece below it are full width, while the vertical side members are cut down in width by the wood's thickness (see step 2). This means that the angled joint between the sides and the crosspiece is not 45°, although it appears so in the pictures (see steps 7 and 8).

The completed surround can be finished with paint, stain or varnish; or it could be given a special paint effect such as marbling or graining.

1 Start by deciding on the precise size and location of the surround. Mark this on the face of the chimney breast (fireplace projection), using a spirit level.

2 Mark the wood thickness on the face of the two uprights. Cut them down in width, using a power saw with a fence or a clamped-on guide.

3 Make up the mantelshelf by nailing lengths of 50 × 25 mm (2 × 1 in) wood to its underside and then pinning on scotia (cove) mouldings as shown.

4 Screw a length of 50 × 25 mm (2 × 1 in) wood on edge to the underside of the mantelshelf. Its length is the width of the surround minus twice the width of the wood.

5 **Right** Fix the support strips. The side strip spacing matches the width of the uprights. The cross strip is placed to match the width of the crosspiece.

BOLSTER CUSHION

CALCULATING FABRIC REQUIREMENTS

Box cushion

Measure the length and width of the top of the pad and add 1.5 cm (½ in) all around for seam allowances. Two pieces of fabric this size are needed, one for the top and one for the bottom of the cover. The gusset is made from four pieces of fabric joined together. Measure the depth and width of the pad and add 1.5 cm (½ in) all around for seam allowances. Cut out three pieces of fabric to this size. Add an extra 3 cm (1 in) to the depth of the fourth piece for the zip seam in the back gusset.

Bolster cushion

To calculate the *length*, measure the bolster from the centre point of one end, along the length and around to the centre point of the opposite end, adding a total of 6 cm (2 in) for hem allowances.

To calculate the *width*, measure the circumference of the pad and add 3 cm (1 in) for seam allowances.

1 Cut out the fabric. Pin and stitch the length of the bolster cover with a French seam (see illustrations). Turn the resulting tube right side out and press the seam.

2 Turn under a double 1.5 cm (½ in) hem at each end of the tube. Pin and tack (baste) in place using a contrasting coloured thread so the stitches are easy to detect.

3 Machine stitch along the hems, keeping the stitching close to the inner folds. Remove the tacking stitches and press thoroughly.

Above: Gathered bolsters contrast well with the more usual rectangular cushion shapes.

4 Using double thread run a row of gathering stitches along each end of the tube, close to the outer fold of the hem and leaving a long thread end. Insert the bolster pad in the tube, then tighten the gathering threads to close the cover. Secure the thread ends, then cover the small hole left at each end by attaching a furnishing tassel, ribbon bow or a covered button.

PIPING

1 Fold a piece of fabric in half diagonally and press the fold. Open out the fabric and using a ruler and pencil, mark out strips parallel to the fold about 4–5 cm (1½–2 in) apart, depending on the thickness of the piping cord. Cut out the strips.

2 Join the strips together with a flat seam to make the required length. Place the piping cord along the centre of the strip, fold it over with wrong sides facing and pin together. Tack (baste) and stitch close to the cord.

3 Lay the covered cord on the right side of the fabric with raw edges aligning and tack in place. Cover with a second piece of fabric, right side downwards and raw edges matching. Stitch the layers together along the seamline using a zip foot on the machine. Remove the tacking stitches.

TABLECLOTHS

Both square and round tablecloths are quick to make. For practical uses choose a washable fabric, either plain or patterned, in a shade which matches or coordinates with the general colour scheme of the room as well as any favourite tableware.

Cotton and synthetic blends are easy to sew, require practically no ironing and so make a good choice for everyday tablecloths in the kitchen or dining room. Plain, heavy cotton and linen look better for more formal occasions, but they require more hard work to keep them looking good over the years. Always treat stains on table linen immediately and launder as soon afterwards as possible.

SQUARE TABLECLOTH

1 Measure the sides of the table top, adding twice the required drop from the edge of the table and 3 cm (1 in) all around for hem allowances. Cut out the fabric. Turn and press a double 1.5 cm (1/2 in) hem around the sides.

Below: Choose a pretty printed fabric to make a covering for a rectangular kitchen or occasional table.

2 Unfold both hems and cut across each corner diagonally, as shown, within 5 mm (1/4 in) of the corner point at the inner fold.

3 Pin the diagonal edges together, with the right sides facing, and stitch a narrow seam 5 mm (1/4 in) from the raw edge. Stitch from the inner corner point and make the seam 1.5 cm (1/2 in) long. Press each seam and turn the corners out to the right side.

4 Re-fold the double hem along the pressed lines. The diagonal seams at each corner make a neat mitre. Pin, tack (baste) and stitch around the edge of the tablecloth, close to the inner fold. Press the hem.

Right: Cover a round occasional table with a floor-length plain undercloth, then top it with a small square cloth made of coordinating fabric.

JOINING FABRIC

When joining fabric to make either a square or round tablecloth, avoid making a seam down the centre as this can look rather unsightly. Instead, cut out two pieces of fabric to the correct width and use one as the central panel. Cut the second piece in half lengthways and join to either side of the panel, matching the pattern if necessary. Use an ordinary flat seam and neaten the raw edges.

ROUND TABLECLOTH

1 Measure the diameter of the table top and add twice the depth of the drop plus 3 cm (1 in) for hem allowances. Make a pattern from dressmaker's pattern paper using a pencil tied to a piece of string measuring half your final measurement. Hold one end of the string down on the paper, pull the string taut and draw a quarter circle on the paper with the pencil. Cut out the pattern.

2 Fold the fabric into four and pin on the quarter circle pattern, aligning the folded edges of the fabric with the straight edges of the paper. Cut out using dressmaker's scissors.

3 Stitch around the outside of the fabric 1.5 cm (1/2 in) from the raw edge. This line of stitching marks the hem edge. Press the edge over onto the wrong side of the fabric along the stitched line without stretching the fabric.

4 Carefully turn under the raw edge to make a double hem, then pin and tack (baste) the hem in place. Stitch around the edge of the tablecloth close to the inner fold of the hem. Press the hem well.

TABLEMATS AND NAPKINS

Tablemats and napkins make the perfect table setting for an informal meal. They are simple to make and can be a good way of using offcuts and remnants of fabric.

Tablemats can be made from plain or patterned fabric and are most effective when machine quilted with a layer of wadding (batting) sandwiched between the top and bottom pieces of fabric. The layers help to protect the table surface beneath the plates. Bind the edges with matching or contrasting fabric or ready-made bias binding. Alternatively, choose ready-quilted fabric and follow the instructions for binding given here to finish the edges.

Napkins are simply a hemmed piece of fabric, usually square and made in a cloth which coordinates with the tablemats or a tablecloth. Give some thought to the practical purpose of napkins and always make them from fabric which is washable. Polyester and cotton blends are a popular choice for informal napkins, but nothing beats the look of pure linen for a formal occasion.

TABLEMAT

1 Decide on the size of the tablemat and cut out two pieces of fabric. Along the short edge of one piece, mark evenly spaced points 2.5 cm (1 in) apart using a ruler and a sharp pencil. Join the points to make lines running across the fabric.

2 Cut a piece of wadding (batting) to the same size as the fabric and sandwich it between the two fabric pieces, with the wrong sides together and the marked piece on top. Pin together carefully, then work rows of tacking (basting) between alternate pencil lines.

3 Lengthen the stitch on the sewing machine slightly, then work parallel rows of machine stitching over the pencil lines using a matching or contrasting thread. Round off the corners by drawing around a cup or small plate, then trim away the surplus fabric.

4 Cut out and join the bias strips until the strip of binding is long enough to go around the edge of the tablemat. Fold the strip so that the raw edges meet in the middle and press. Open out one folded edge of the binding and pin it around the tablemat with the right sides facing and raw edges aligning. Neatly fold back the raw edges where the binding meets. Stitch along the crease of the binding.

5 Fold over the binding to the wrong side of the tablemat. Pin and stitch the binding in place by hand as shown. Turn the tablemat to the right side and strengthen the edge by working one row of machine stitching around the edge close to the inside fold of the binding.

SIZES AND FABRIC REQUIREMENTS

Tablemats
To decide on a suitable size for tablemats, first arrange a place setting with two sizes of plate plus cutlery (flatware) and measure the area these cover. The side plate and glass can be placed on the table at the edge of the mat, if preferred.

Traditionally, rectangular tablemats measure approximately 20 × 30 cm (8 × 12 in), but they can be larger – up to 30 × 45 cm (12 × 18 in). Having decided on the finished size of the tablemats, allow at least 5 cm (2 in)

extra all around for working the quilting. Always trim the surplus fabric away after completing the machine quilting but before beginning to bind the edges.

Napkins
Napkins are usually square and vary in size from small napkins of 30 cm (12 in) square for tea or coffee parties to large ones measuring 60 cm (24 in) for formal occasions. However, a good all-purpose size for napkins is 40 cm (16 in) square.

3 Next, mark up and cut the components to width, using a circular saw with a fence or a guide strip clamped across it to keep the cuts perfectly straight.

4 Mark the height of the uprights and the length of the shelves required on the components. Square a cutting line across them, using a try square.

7 Stand the unit against the back of the wardrobe or alcove. Mark the position of the lower shelf supports on it. Cut notches to fit the supports.

8 Reposition the central shelf unit, then lay the lower shelf on its supports. Nail or screw down through it into the supports and the shelf unit.

9 Fit hangers to support the clothes rail beneath the lower shelf. Add a second lower rail if wished. Complete the unit by adding the top shelf.

MAKING UTILITY SHELVING

Storage space in workshops, garages, basements and attics is best provided by building simple but sturdy shelves from inexpensive materials. Use wood that is sawn, not planed (dressed), for the framework, and cut the shelves from scrap plywood. Damaged boards and offcuts are often available cheaply from timber merchants (lumberyards).

The shelving units shown here are made from 50 mm (2 in) square wood, with shelves of 19 mm (³/4 in) plywood. The only other materials needed are some scraps of 9 mm (³/8 in) thick plywood for the small triangular braces that help to stiffen the structure.

Start by working out how big the unit is to be. Uprights should be spaced about 760 mm (2 ft 6 in) apart so that the shelves will not sag; they can reach right up to ceiling level if desired. Match the depth of the unit to what is to be stored and to the amount of space available. Remember that it can be difficult reaching things at the back of deep shelves. After measuring up and estimating how many uprights and shelves are needed, buy all the materials and start work.

Make the uprights like a ladder, with glued and nailed butt joints reinforced with plywood triangles measuring about

100 mm (4 in) along the edges forming the right angle. Space the horizontals to suit storage requirements and cut plywood shelves to fit.

Stand the uprights against the wall at the appropriate spacing and screw them to the wall – either into the wall studs, or into wall plugs or masonry anchors if it is solid masonry. Then cut the shelves to length; each 'rung' of the ladder will support two shelves except at the ends of the run, so cut the latter to span between the centres of the rungs. Notch the shelf corners so that they fit around the uprights and are locked in place.

1 Start by deciding on the height the uprights should be, and on how many 'ladders' are needed. Cut them all to length with a power saw.

2 Make up the ladders by gluing and nailing the rungs between pairs of uprights. Reinforce the joints by gluing and screwing on plywood triangles.

3 Stand the assembled ladders against the wall, check that they are truly vertical, and screw them to the wall – into wooden studs or masonry anchors.

4 Cut as many plywood shelves as are needed so they span between the centre lines of the rungs; notch the corners so they will fit neatly around the uprights.

MAKING A TOOL CABINET

This tool storage rack is basically a wall-mounted backing board of 19 mm (³/4 in) thick plywood. Tools are hung on various supports, as shown in the illustration. These are located in, and slide along, horizontal channels formed by pinning 38 mm (1 ¹/2 in) wide strips of 12 mm (¹/2 in) plywood to the backing panel and then pinning 75 × 19 mm (3 × ³/4 in) softwood strips to the plywood. Make the trays for small tools from 12 mm (¹/2 in) plywood, and use hardwood dowel pegs or old wire coat hangers to make support hooks for larger tools. Slide the back plate of each support into its channel at the sides of the rack, and move them along to where they are needed.

MAKING A GARAGE STORAGE WALL

The garage is a favourite place to store all manner of things, including tools and materials for do-it-yourself, gardening and car maintenance. Unless these are kept under control, they will spill over until there is no room for the car. The solution is to build a shallow full-height storage unit along either the side or the end wall of the garage, tailor-made to suit whatever will be stored there.

The design concept of the storage wall is quite simple, and is based around creating bays offering different storage facilities. One can have floor-to-ceiling shelves, another a drawer system using plastic washing-up bowls (washbowls) sliding on wooden support strips. The next bay can offer full-height open storage for stepladders and scaffold boards, and another wider one provides space to store sheet materials neatly on edge beneath a wall-mounted rack for hanging up things such as a portable workbench or a set of car ramps. Simply select whatever types of bay are needed, and arrange them in any order.

The structure is based on ladder frames fixed to the wall to support shelves, drawers and whatever else is required. The frame is made mainly from 50 mm (2 in) square sawn softwood, with 75 × 25 mm (3 × 1 in) wood for the shelves and the slatted hanging rack. The hinged section drops down to allow sheets of plywood and the like to be placed on edge behind it, and is held shut with a simple hasp and staple at each side. The wall-mounted rack allows heavy items to be hung out of the way yet readily to hand on metal S-hooks.

1 Start by securing the uprights to the garage wall to form the various bays. Check that each is vertical before fixing it in place.

2 Set sole plates on something damp-proof (here sheet vinyl flooring), and screw them down into wall plugs in holes drilled in the garage floor.

3 Simply nail components together as required to form the frames making up each bay. Add horizontals to support shelves or plastic bowl drawers.

4 To make up the drop-down flap for the sheet materials storage bay, hinge the two front uprights to their baseplates and add a cross rail.

5 To make up the wall rack, nail on the slats, using an offcut as a spacer. Make the shelves in the same way, nailing the slats to 50 × 25 mm (2 × 1 in) bearers.

3 Choose a wall plug sized to match the screw being used, and push it into the hole until its rim is flush with the wall. Tap it with a hammer if necessary.

4 Thread the screw through a clearance hole drilled in the object being fixed, insert it in the mouth of the wall plug and drive it home.

5 Alternatively, use long-sleeved frame plugs. Drill holes through the wood and into the wall, insert the plug and tighten the screw to make the fixing.

MAKING FIXINGS INTO STUDS

1 Use an electronic stud finder to locate the stud or ceiling joist positions. It works by detecting the nails which secure the plasterboard (gypsum board).

2 When the stud or joist positions are marked, drill clearance holes in the object to be fixed at matching centres. Check these for accuracy.

3 Drill pilot holes through the board surface and into the stud or joist. Make sure that the drill bit is at right angles to the surface.

4 Insert screws in all the clearance holes, then offer up the object, align it with the pre-drilled holes and drive the screws home.

ADHESIVES, MASTICS AND REPAIR TAPES

There is a huge range of adhesives available nowadays. Their labelling is now generally much clearer than it was a few years ago, so finding the right product is considerably easier than it used to be. Here is a guide to the types that are likely to be needed for most repair jobs.

General-purpose adhesives

These are clear solvent-based adhesives which will stick paper and cardboard, wood, leather and a few types of plastic such as solid polystyrene and ABS. They are used straight from the tube. Check the instructions carefully; some recommend applying the adhesive to both surfaces, others to just one. Whichever method is used, hold or clamp the repair for a while; the adhesive takes some time after assembly to gain full strength. The joint is generally not heat-resistant and may not be water-resistant either. Adhesive can be removed from fingers, or anywhere else it gets by mistake, with cellulose thinner, acetone or nail varnish remover – but the last will attack gloss paint, french polish, some varnishes, and any plastic that the adhesive will stick.

Adhesives for wood

The most widely used type of adhesive for general woodwork is *PVA woodworking adhesive*, often referred to as 'white glue'. It will bond softwood, hardwood and all manufactured boards, and is colourless when dry; spills can be wiped away with a damp cloth before the adhesive sets. The joint must be clamped until the adhesive hardens – for a couple of hours at least – to get the best results. Exposure to damp will weaken the adhesive and cause failure. If such exposure is likely, be sure to use one of the cross-linking versions which give a high degree of water resistance.

Adhesives for laminates

Plastic laminates, flexible sheet materials such as foam and leather, and vinyl or cork floor tiles are stuck in place with a *contact adhesive*. This is spread on both surfaces and is allowed to become touch-dry before the two are pressed together. The resulting bond is instant, and cannot normally be repositioned; but some kinds offer a degree of slip – they are often called *thixotropic adhesives*. Contact adhesive is also moderately heatproof and water-resistant.

Most contact adhesives are solvent-based, and the fumes are both inflammable and noxious to inhale, so work with good ventilation and no naked lights. Clean up spills with the manufacturer's own solvent, cellulose thinner, acetone or nail varnish remover. Water-based contact adhesives are also available, and these are much safer and more pleasant to use; spills can be removed while still wet with a damp cloth.

Adhesives for plastics

Some plastics are very difficult to stick with adhesives. Two which cannot be stuck by any means are polythene (polyethylene) and polypropylene, the bendy plastics used for such things are washing-up bowls (wash bowls) and buckets; they must be fused by heat. Flexible PVC – used for seat covers, sunbeds and beach balls, for example – can be stuck with special *vinyl repair adhesive*. *Polystyrene cement* or general-purpose adhesive will mend rigid polystyrene – used for some kitchen and bathroom accessories – and the similar but tougher ABS. Do not use it for expanded polystyrene ceiling tiles or coving (crown molding), though, as

SILICONE MASTIC Use silicone mastic to seal around bathroom fittings. Push the nozzle along the gap so it leaves a neat concave finish to the mastic bead.

ACRYLIC MASTIC Use acrylic mastic indoors and frame sealant outdoors to seal gaps between wood and masonry where a rigid filler would tend to crack and fall out.

REPAIR TAPE Use repair tapes to make temporary repairs to cracked glass, or to waterproof glazing bars on glass roofs. Simply press the tape into place.

FITTING THIN-FILM DOUBLE GLAZING

1 Start by sticking lengths of double-sided adhesive tape to the window frame, about 12 mm ($^1/_2$ in) in from the surrounding masonry.

2 Press the film onto the tape, pulling it as taut as possible. Then play hot air from a hair-drier over it to tighten it up and pull out any wrinkles.

3 When the film is even and wrinkle-free, trim off the excess film all the way around the window with a sharp utility knife.

5 When positioning the bottom track on the window sill, use a straightedge and a spirit level to check that it is perfectly aligned with the top track.

6 Measure up for the glass as directed in the kit manufacturer's instructions, and order the glass. Fit cut lengths of glazing gasket to the edges of each pane.

7 Fit the first pane into the track by inserting its top edge in the top channel, and then lowering its bottom edge. Repeat the procedure for the other pane.

DRAUGHTPROOFING

Ill fitting windows and doors are a major source of heat loss, as well as causing cold draughts. Fitting efficient draught stripping around them will reduce the losses and cut down the draughts, and is a simple job to carry out. Modern self-adhesive foams are much more efficient and longer-lasting than older types, and are ideal for windows, while doors and sash windows are best draughtproofed with pin-on (tack-on) plastic or sprung metal strips

or types containing a compressible rubber seal. Special draught excluders are available for door thresholds (saddles), and can be fitted to the door bottom or across the threshold. There are even excluders designed to fit over letter plate openings.

Remember that draughtproofing a home will close off many 'unofficial' sources of ventilation, turning it into a well sealed box. Fuel-burning appliances such as boilers and room

heaters must have an adequate source of fresh air to burn safely, so it is wise to ask a fuel supplier to check that there is adequate ventilation in rooms containing such appliances. Often a ventilator in a window pane will solve the problem. Efficient draughtproofing may also increase condensation, especially in kitchens and bathrooms. This can be prevented by providing controlled ventilation in these rooms with an extractor fan.

DRAUGHTPROOFING DOORS

1 The simplest type of door-bottom draught excluder is a brush seal mounted in a wood or plastic strip. Simply cut it to length and screw it on to the foot of the door.

2 Alternatively, fit a threshold (saddle) strip. Cut the metal bar to length and screw it to the sill, then fit the compressible rubber sealing strip in the channel.

3 Draughtproof a letter plate opening by screwing on a special brush seal. Check that it does not foul the letter plate flap if this opens inwards.

4 Draughtproof the sides and top of the door frame by pinning (tacking) on lengths of plastic or sprung metal sealing strip. Pin the edge farthest from the door stop bead.

5 Alternatively, stick lengths of self-adhesive foam excluder to the stop bead against which the door closes. At the hinge side, stick it to the frame.

6 A third option is to use lengths of self-adhesive brush strip excluder. These three types can also be used for draughtproofing hinged casement windows.

DRAUGHTPROOFING SASH WINDOWS

1 To fit sprung metal strip excluder to a sliding sash window, first prise off the staff bead (window stop) that holds the inner sash in position, and swing it out.

2 Measure the length of strip needed to fit the height of the window, and cut it to length with scissors. Beware the sharp edges of the metal.

3 Pin (tack) the strip to the side of the frame so it will press against the edge of the sliding sash. Pin it through the edge facing towards the room.

4 Use the special wheeled springing tool provided with the excluder to make a small groove in the strip, causing it to spring outwards.

5 Pin a strip along the inner face of the top sash meeting rail (mullion), and 'spring' it so it presses against the outer face of the bottom sash rail.

6 Draughtproof the bottom edge of the lower sash and the top edge of the upper one by sticking on lengths of self-adhesive foam excluder.

PROVIDING CONTROLLABLE VENTILATION

In every house stale, moist air must be removed and replaced with fresh air from outside. This happens not only in an obvious way when a window is opened or an extractor fan switched on, but all the time. For example, air passes up chimney flues, or finds a way out through the inevitable small gaps in the house structure.

Unless power ventilated, most modern houses have very little chance of such ventilation because improved standards of insulation and draughtproofing have made them much more airtight than formerly. Of course

this reduces heating bills and keeps the house's occupants warm and comfortable, as long as they do not create too much moisture for the air to hold. If they do, condensation will be the inevitable result, and extra ventilation will be needed.

This reduction in natural ventilation not only causes trouble within the house, it can also affect its structure. Two particular problem areas are roof spaces and under-floor voids. To prevent it, more ventilation must be provided via ridge and eaves-level vents in roofs, and airbricks in walls.

For ventilating rooms, what is needed is some controllable means of getting rid of excess moist air without wasting too much valuable heat. In habitually steamy rooms such as kitchens and bathrooms, an extractor fan is the best solution. It will extract the moist air quickly, and will also help to get rid of unwanted smells. In other rooms, fitting small 'trickle' ventilators at the top of window frames and putting in extra airbricks will often supply enough ventilation to allow the moist air to disperse before condensation becomes a problem.

FITTING AN EXTRACTOR FAN

1 Decide on the fan position, then mark the outline of the ducting on the wall outside. Drill holes right through the wall to mark it on the inside too.

2 Drill a series of closely spaced holes through the wall from inside, working within the guide holes drilled from outside. Repeat on the wall outside.

3 Chop out the brickwork with a wide bolster (stonecutter's chisel) and club (spalling) hammer, again working from inside and outside the house.

4 Use ducting for a cooker hood. Line the hole with a short length of pipe, then use connectors as required to connect the hood to the outlet.

5 Wall-mounted fans usually need a round hole. Cut it out, line it with a short length of sleeving and make good around it inside and outside the house.

6 Fit the fan into the sleeving, ready for its electrical supply to be connected. Fit a cover grille to the outside end of the ducting.

WINDOWS

Basement, balcony, or bedsit – whatever the style of your home and whatever you're looking to achieve, you'll to find something here to revolutionize your windows. So, if you thought it was all just plastic curtain hooks and tracks, read on! All you have to do is invest in a staple gun and some inexpensive fittings and fixings, and follow our simple step-by-step instructions to show you exactly how to make your windows the fabulous focal point of each room. You will never look in curtain (drape) departments again once you have been shown our instant window makeovers and realize how easy it is to create stunning and dramatic effects.

The ideas in this book will carry you away from traditional methods and old-fashioned styles towards the freshness and freedom of experimental window dressing. Many of our projects were inspired by looking at familiar materials in a new light, such as using grass beach mats for blinds (shades) or tartan wool rugs for an imposing curtain. There are all kinds of materials that can make the leap from their everyday practical uses to highly original ones. This chapter contains projects to suit every taste and every budget including quick stylish ideas for tie-backs, hanging treatments and colour schemes and simple effects created by draping, typing, stapling, buttoning, hanging, clipping and glueing all kinds of fabrics. You will probably come up with your own ideas and variations on our themes, too.

So, armed with these innovative ideas, take a fresh look at the windows around your home and have lots of fun transforming them to reflect your personality. The real beauty of our quick and inexpensive window dressing creations is that, if you happen to change your mind at a later date, you can simply come up with another one!

Opposite: A new drape at the window can be all it takes to lift a newly designed room and make it feel more homely.

EGYPTIAN DREAM

A PAIR OF COTTON SHEETS makes the most wonderful drape and all the seams are perfectly finished. The bigger the sheets, the more luxurious and elegant the window will look – drapes should always be generous. Wooden clothes pegs (pins) can be wedged into a piece of old wooden floor-boarding or driftwood – if you drill the holes at an angle, the fixing will be stronger as well as more decorative.

YOU WILL NEED

scissors

cotton tape, 2.5m (2½yd)

2 flat king-size cotton sheets

needle and white sewing thread

drill

length of floorboarding or driftwood, window width plus 15cm (6in) either side

6 old-fashioned wooden clothes pegs (pins)

spirit level

wall plugs (plastic anchors) and screws

screwdriver

1 With scissors, cut the cotton tape into six strips of equal length.

2 Divide the width of each sheet top by three and use the divisions as points to attach the tapes. Fold each tape in half and use small stitches to sew them to the top of the sheet.

3 Drill six holes at equal distances along the floorboarding and wedge in the pegs (pins). Drill a hole either end of the floorboarding and screw it into the wall, using a spirit level to check it is straight, and appropriate fixings to secure it.

4 Tie the tapes securely and neatly to the pegs and arrange the drapes.

POT-POURRI

THIS IS AN EXTREMELY QUICK and effective way to trim the top edge of a loop-headed curtain (drape). Tie ribbons round the loops and hang a selection of decorations from them. Here we have used pieces of pot-pourri but you could also use odd earrings, bells, tin stars, buttons and so on. If you have a pinch-pleated or a simple gathered curtain heading, a small bow or knot with ribbon hanging down would look effective.

YOU WILL NEED

tape measure

1cm (½in) wide hessian (burlap) or linen

ribbon or tape

dressmaker's scissors

needle and matching sewing thread (optional)

pot-pourri

glue gun and glue sticks

1 Decide the appropriate length or lengths of ribbon or tape needed in relation to the drop of the curtain (drape), so they look in proportion.

2 Cut the ribbon or tape to length and cut the ends at an angle, so they look neat. If you are using a ribbon that frays, hem the ends. Select the pieces of pot-pourri that most complement one another. Using a glue gun, attach the pieces of pot-pourri to the ends of the ribbon or tape.

3 Tie the ribbon or tape to the curtain loops. It is best not to fix them permanently, so you can change the design when you wish and take them off when you wash the curtains.

WHITE MISCHIEF

SMALL DETAILS SUCH AS the curtain (drape) clips in this project make the important difference between an obvious and an elegant solution to curtain hanging. The white muslin (cheesecloth) is a generously long piece, folded in half, allowing a drop 1½ times the length of the window – it really is a very simple, yet elegant example of window dressing! Small brass curtain clips fit over the rail and catch the muslin along the fold.

YOU WILL NEED

dowel, window width
woodstain
kitchen cloth
drill
wall plugs (plastic anchors) and nails
hammer
curtain (drape) clips
white muslin (cheesecloth)
wooden spear or a garden implement

1 Stain the length of dowel by shaking woodstain on to a soft cloth and rubbing the dowel with it until you achieve the effect you want.

2 Drill two holes either side of the window and insert the wall plugs (plastic anchors). Bang in the nails.

3 Clip the muslin (cheesecloth) along the fold, leaving an equal distance between the clips. Thread the rings on to the dowel and place the dowel over the nails.

4 Spread the rings along the dowel so that the muslin falls in even drapes.

5 Knot the front drop of muslin on to the end of the spear and prop this across the window.

SHELL TIE-BACKS

CURTAIN (DRAPE) TIE-BACKS can be made in a tremendously wide range of styles so you can use them to create whatever decorative effect you like. Though we normally think of a simple braid or tassel, tie-backs can be trimmed to make them focal- and talking-points within the room. Here a fishing net was festooned with different types and sizes of shells. You could wire a mass of very small shells on to the net or even edge the curtain with a widely spaced line of matching shells.

YOU WILL NEED

fishing net

shells

fine wire

wire cutters

glue gun and glue sticks
or electric drill, with very
fine drill bit

string (optional)

1 Take the fishing net and arrange it in graceful folds. Gather together a mass of shells and see how they look best when arranged on the net. Cut lengths of fine wire. These can then be glued to the back of the shells so that they can be wired on to the netting.

2 Alternatively, drill holes in the shells. Thread string through the holes for attaching to the net.

3 Fix the shells on the netting. Make another tie-back in the same way. Loop the tie-backs around the curtains and on to the wall.

ROBINSON CRUSOE BLINDS

THIS REALLY MUST BE one of the cheapest, simplest, yet most effective blind (shade) solutions ever: it involves two grass beach mats, three cup hooks, a length of rope and some brass paper fasteners. The beach mats are made with coloured tape binding, and as they are extremely light-weight, they can be rolled up by hand and tied with rope. Measure your window carefully – the mats are available in one width only, so they are not suitable for all types and sizes of window.

YOU WILL NEED

bradawl

3 cup hooks

2 grass beach mats

paper fasteners

rope

scissors

1 Make three holes with a bradawl, one either side and one in the middle of the window recess. Screw in the cup hooks.

2 Make a channel for the rope at the top of the blind by folding over the mat 4cm (1½in) and securing with a row of evenly spaced paper fasteners, pushed through and folded back.

3 Knot the rope on to one of the cup hooks, leaving a tail hanging about a third of the way down the window. Thread the rope through the blind (shade) and pull it tight before knotting it on to the middle hook. Cut the rope the same length as before.

4 Cut a length of rope twice the length of the window drop and knot it in the middle, on to the middle hook. Roll up the blind by hand and tie the two ends of this rope to hold it at the required height. Repeat this process with a second length of rope for the second blind.

ARTIST'S STUDIO

THIS IS THE IDEAL WAY to cover a large studio window, and as canvas comes in so many sizes, you're bound to find a piece to fit your window. If you have never previously considered the possibility of becoming a painter, then this is a good way to start – curtains (drapes) can also be art! Here, chalks were used to draw on to the canvas and change the flat panel into a boldly gathered backdrop. You could use this idea as your inspiration, or you could flick colours on it in Jackson Pollock style, or simply add a few minimalist squiggles. If your window receives a lot of light, you may want to suspend a builder's dust-sheet (drop cloth) in front of the window. This will provide a lining for the main curtain.

YOU WILL NEED

canvas, 1½ × window width

chalks or acrylic paints and paintbrush

drill

4 chunky garage hooks

screwdriver

metal cleat

rope

double-sided carpet tape

brass eyelets

hammer

1 Draw, paint or print on to the canvas using whatever style or design you have chosen – the bolder the better, as the canvas will cover a large surface area.

2 Fix the garage hooks securely into the wall above the window, spaced at equal intervals.

3 Screw the cleat to the wall, about halfway down the side of the window, then wind one end of the rope around it several times.

4 Take the long end of the rope up and through the hooks along the top.

5 Pull the rope taut and tie it on to the end hook. Then fix the seams and eyelets on to the canvas following the manufacturer's instructions.

6 Thread the rope through the first eyelet from behind, allowing about 16cm (6¼in) between the hook and the eyelet. Then, leaving the same distance again, twist a loop in the rope and put it on the hook.

7 Take the rope down and through the back of the next eyelet, then up and over the back taut rope, which now forms a 'rail' for the rope to rest on.

8 When you reach the end of the curtain, take the rope through the last hook.

9 Take the rope straight down the side of the window and tie it neatly on to the cleat. ➤

10 Cut an extra length of rope and hook it over one of the top centre hooks so that one length falls to the front and the other to the back of the canvas. Gather the canvas up and get hold of both ends of the rope. Tie these together in a knot and leave the ends dangling free.

Above: The knot holding the curtain back from the window allows the light to come through.

Above: Allow plenty of canvas so that it spills generously out on to the floor below the window.

Above: The knotted rope forms an additional decorative element in its own right.

Above: The natural colour of the canvas enhances the subtle colours of the design.

SCOTLAND THE BRAVE

HERE IS THE PERFECT WAY to show off bright tartan wool rugs. Draped and pinned over a wooden rail, they will add a baronial touch to the plainest of windows. Tartan has quite a masculine feel and looks good alongside old leather cases and other "practical" accessories. This window would suit a study or hallway with plain walls, contrasting with the richness and pattern of the tartan. Fix the curtain rail above the window, extending about 30cm (12in) each side.

YOU WILL NEED

wooden curtain rail
spirit level
drill
wall plugs (plastic anchors) and screws
screwdriver
3 different coloured
tartan rugs
6 kilt pins

1 Fix the wooden rail according to the pack instructions. Begin on the left with one corner of a rug. Take the corner over from the back and pin it about 30cm (12in) down the rug.

2 Drape the second rug over the rail, also on the left, but arrange it so that the drape is more or less equal at the front and back. Lift it in places and pin it on to the first rug using kilt pins.

3 Drape the third tartan rug along the rest of the pole diagonally so that the fringed edge can be seen hanging down from the right corner. Lift sections of this rug and pin it in drapes by attaching it with kilt pins to the second rug.

4 Stand back and check the effect, then use any remaining pins to hold the rugs in place, making a feature of the fringing and the pins.

HANGING AROUND

MAKE THE PRETTIEST of chandelier-hangings with simple deciduous twigs such as apple or pear branches. Select a few branches with gnarled, interesting shapes and bind them together to make a pleasing structure, then hang the finished chandelier in the centre of a window suspended from a length of gold cord. Trim the branches with eye-catching trinkets such as crystal droplets and tiny pearls, all fixed with the finest of gold twine. This project would also look stunning hanging from a ceiling rose or as a wall decoration.

YOU WILL NEED

2–3 apple or pear tree branches

fine gold wire

scissors

gold cord

crystal droplets

gold beading wire

small pearls

gilded decorations

1 Take the branches and move them around until they form a pretty shape. Bind the branches together at the top with fine gold wire.

2 Attach a length of gold cord to hang the branches.

3 Thread crystal droplets on to gold wire. Make short strings of pearls.

4 Wire the remaining decorations, then twist the wires to make hanging loops. Position the twig chandelier and hang on the jewels.

BROWN PAPER PANELLING

BROWN WRAPPING PAPER has its own characteristic colour and texture, which look quite wonderful on walls. You can buy it on large rolls, which make papering under a dado rail simplicity itself. Here, the brown paper has been combined with gum arabic adhesive tape for an unusual and elegant interpretation of a classic interior look. You could also add a simple skirting (base) board, using 5 × 2.5cm (2 × 1in) timber.

YOU WILL NEED

brown wrapping paper
wallpaper paste
pasting brush
plumb line
pencil
straight edge
paintbrush
gum arabic adhesive
paper roll
spirit level
black beading
glue gun and glue sticks

1 Stick the brown wrapping paper, matt (flat) side inwards, to the wall. Use wallpaper paste, as for wallpaper.

2 Use a plumb line and straight edge to mark vertical guidelines for the stripes on the brown paper. With a paintbrush, wet the wall in a stripe the width of the gum arabic tape and stick the tape down. Make sure you cover up all the guidelines.

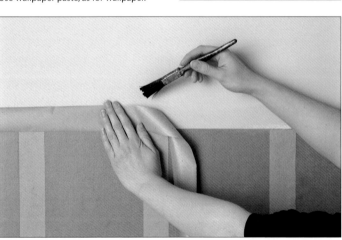

3 Use a spirit level and straight edge to draw a horizontal guideline for the under-dado border. Stick the tape in place in the same way.

4 Attach the beading along the top of the border, using the glue gun.

CORK-STAMPED FLOOR

THIS PRETTY STAMP has been made from seven wine bottle corks. They have been taped together in a daisy shaped bundle and the pattern shapes are cut from the surface of the cork bundle with a scalpel. Dense cork like this is a good material to carve into, being both soft and very smooth. Use the stamp on dust-free sanded wood, or on cork tiles with a dark woodstain. Allow it to stand and soak up the stain for ten minutes then blot it on kitchen paper before you begin printing. Use the paper strips to ensure that the pattern is an even distance from the wall.

YOU WILL NEED

7 wine bottle corks
wood glue or PVA (white) glue
strong adhesive tape
felt-tipped pen
scalpel
2 paper strips of equal width
dark woodstain
bowl
kitchen paper

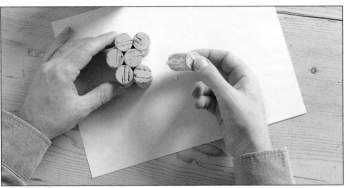

1 Glue the corks in a daisy formation, standing the ends flat on a piece of paper. This will provide a level printing surface. Bind the corks together with strong adhesive tape once the glue has become tacky.

2 Draw the pattern onto the cork surface with a felt-tipped pen. Cut out the background pieces with a scalpel.

3 Start by making one stamp at each corner, placing the paper spacing strips against the skirting (base) boards.

4 Move the strips along the straight skirting (base) board section and stamp a motif halfway between the first two. Stamp a row of evenly spaced motifs between the existing prints. Continue to stamp a border all round the room.

3 When dry, gently sand until you have a level surface.

4 Paint the whole surface white and allow it to dry.

5 Paint over the whole surface of the floor in dark grey.

6 Using a candle, apply a generous coating of wax with circular movements to the surface of the floor.

7 Take off most of the candle wax, using a scraper.

8 Follow this with a coat of mid-grey emulsion (latex) paint. ➤

9 Apply another coat of wax. Take off the wax with the scraper.

10 Apply white paint with a dry softening brush, to soften the whole effect. Seal with matt (flat) varnish. If you are surrounding the MDF with cork tiles, lay them at the end and butt up to the edges neatly.

RUBBER MATS

AVAILABLE FROM RUBBER MANUFACTURERS, this safety matting is valued for its non-slip and protective qualities, and since it is waterproof, it is particularly useful in, say, a shower room. Rubber matting doesn't fray when cut and will happily absorb any lumps or strange joins in a floor. Clean and seal the matting with a silicone spray polish, then fix it in place using any rubber contact adhesive. Make sure your floor is sanded, or lay an MDF (medium-density fiberboard) layer underneath before starting.

YOU WILL NEED

2 types of rubber safety mat

tape measure

metal rule or straight edge

craft knife

Pirelli rubber tiles in
different patterns

rubber contact adhesive

WD-40 or silicone spray

1 Measure the floor and the rubber matting and carefully trim the matting to size.

2 For the corners, cut four squares. Divide these diagonally and make four squares by placing two triangles together, with the grooves running across and top to bottom. Position these and the runners around the edge of the room.

3 Cut pieces from the other matting to fit the central section. Cut the tiles into squares, then cut holes in the mat at regular intervals to take the squares.

4 Secure all the pieces with rubber adhesive, applied to both surfaces. Spray with WD-40 or silicone spray.

STENCILLED HARDBOARD

DAMAGED OR IRREGULAR FLOORS are frequently covered in hardboard and you may feel that this smooth, hard surface is especially in keeping if you have adopted a modernist, minimalist approach to decorating. If you discover hardboard in mint condition, in most instances it is not wise to lift it, as it is probably hiding some horror below. However, with several coats of varnish, hardboard has a natural patina of its own, which is very appealing and works as a neutral background as well as a wooden floor does. Introduce additional interest by using stencils, which here mimic a rather fifties-style rug, although the brown hardboard would suit different colours. The contrast of black or white works well; choose a bold, non-figurative pattern.

YOU WILL NEED

metal ruler or straight edge

pencil

paper

black water-based paint

paintbrushes

masking tape

self-healing cutting mat

acetate sheet

craft knife

pin

stencil brush

lint-free cloth or fine-grade abrasive paper (optional)

eraser

gloss varnish

1 Draw the border motif to the desired size on paper.

2 Photocopy the design and make sure that the repeat works, by placing several sheets together.

3 Work out a right-angled section for the corners. Make sure it ties in neatly with the repeat on both sides.

4 Black in the design and photocopy it. Lay the copies around the floor, to ensure that your design will fit pleasingly, and experiment until you have an effect you are happy with.

5 With a pencil, mark the outer edge of your border on the floor (in the photograph, this is about 13cm (5½in) from the edge of the room).

6 Draw out pencil guidelines for your border all round the room.

7 Stick one of the photocopies, with masking tape, to the cutting mat. Tape the acetate sheet over it.

8 Using the steel ruler and holding the knife at an angle, carefully cut out the stencil. To help get neat, sharp corners, make a pin prick just at the corner first; this also helps to prevent you from cutting too far.

9 With masking tape, attach the stencil to the hardboard, lining it up carefully with your guidelines.

10 Using a stencil brush, stipple in the neat black triangles, making sure that the paint is very dry so that it does not seep under the stencil. ➤

11 Lift up the stencil and re-position it for the next section. Remember to make sure the underside of the stencil is clear of paint. If you need to mask certain areas of the stencil so that you continue the repeat when working the corners, do this with a piece of paper held firmly in place with masking tape.

12 If you make a mistake or smudge the stencilling, rub it clean with a damp cloth or, if the surface is more porous, very gently sand away the paint when dry. Finally, remove the guidelines with an eraser and seal the floor with at least two coats of varnish.

POP-ART FLOOR

MUCH INSPIRATION for interior decoration is to be gleaned from the pop artists of this century, with their whimsical approach to art. These naïve shapes painted on a large surface make use of the pop-art conventions of boldness and simplicity, with multiple repetitions of strong images rather than intricate busyness. Dramatically discordant colours – orange and shocking pink in this case – are the most appropriate. This idea works best on a concrete floor.

YOU WILL NEED

white matt (flat) emulsion (latex) paint

paint roller

tape measure

pencil

masking tape

blue, red, shocking pink and orange matt (flat) emulsion (latex) paint

PVA (white) glue or acrylic varnish

1 Give the floor two coats of white paint, to ensure that the colours of the design ring bright and true.

2 Measure and draw out your design. Mask off the border, which needs to be crisply painted. Do the same along the outside of the star.

3 Paint the star, then fill in the area inside the border; masking may not be necessary as a little white space between the star and border and background makes it look as though silk-screening has been used – a technique common in pop art. Seal with diluted PVA (white) glue or acrylic varnish.

STUDDED FLOOR

CREATE THE APPEARANCE of the deck of a battleship in your bathroom, with studs positioned at regular intervals across the floor and painted in battleship grey. Alternatively, you could leave the wood natural and studs unpainted. The broad silver studs used here are called "domes of silence", because they are designed to fit under chair legs to help them glide smoothly across the floor without making a noise. However, you can choose any studs, as long as they are sturdy enough to withstand the traffic on the floor and they are not sharp or liable to damage shoes or furniture. Sand the floor carefully before commencing.

YOU WILL NEED
pencil
steel ruler or straight edge
studs or "domes of silence"
eraser
acrylic varnish (optional)
paintbrush (optional)
tack hammer
cloth, softwood block or
carpet scrap
wood glue (optional)

1 Decide on the spacing and pattern of the studs or domes. Draw diagonal grid lines in accordance with your design and mark with a little cross where each stud is to go.

2 Rub out all markings, except the crosses. If necessary, apply a couple of coats of acrylic varnish to the whole floor, to seal the wood.

3 Using a hammer and something soft, such as a folded cloth or softwood block, to prevent damage to the studs, hammer them in over the crosses. If you use "domes of silence", which have relatively shallow teeth, hammer them in only half way to start with. Remove the domes, apply a little wood glue and then replace them and hammer them in all the way. This technique can be used on any decorative wooden floor.

BEACH MAT BED

A SIMPLE FOUR-POSTER FRAME can be built to fit around an existing base and mattress. Only basic carpentry skills are required, as the timber can be cut to size when you buy it, and just needs drilling and screwing together. The wood used here is basic construction timber that has been left in its natural state, but you could colour it with wood stain or paint it to co-ordinate with the decor of the bedroom. Grass beach mats are perfect for hanging around the four-poster, especially if your room is decorated with natural fabrics and earth colours. The loosely stitched grass strips allow a soothing, soft golden light to filter through and the air to circulate.

YOU WILL NEED

grass beach mats

packet of brass paper fasteners

rough twine

scissors

odd-shaped shells, pebbles and driftwood

1 Fold one short edge of each beach mat over the top rail of the four-poster frame. Push paper fasteners through the mats just below the rail and open out the prongs. Use four fasteners along the top of each beach mat.

2 The mats are edged with different coloured tape that makes fine stripes around the bed. Arrange the mats to make the most of this striping.

3 Decide how many blinds you want to tie up – maybe all, or just a select few. You will need about 1 m (1 yd) of rough twine for each mat to be rolled up. Cut the lengths required and tie some shells, pebbles and bits of driftwood randomly along the length and at each end of the twine.

4 Dangle the ties over the top rail and use them to hold back the rolled-up blinds.

TARTAN BEDHEAD

WOOLLEN TARTAN RUGS are comfort blankets, traditionally used on winter car journeys and picnics. The two rugs used in this project are doubled over, with their folded edges meeting in the middle. To complete the Highland hunting lodge atmosphere, the rugs are hung above the bedhead from a rough-hewn "branch".

YOU WILL NEED

2 matching tartan blankets or rugs

tape measure

needle

thick contrasting thread

2.5cm (1in) wooden dowel (slightly longer than the bed width)

craft knife

fine-grade abrasive paper

cloth

shellac

2 iron pipe holders (to fit 2.5cm (1in) pipe)

drill and wallplugs

screwdriver

kilt pins

1 Fold each blanket in half lengthways and pin together along the folded seam. Blanket stitch the outside edges, then stitch the blankets together along the folded edge. If you don't like sewing, hold the seams closed with three kilt pins.

2 Start decorating the wooden pole by roughly carving away both ends of the dowel with a craft knife. Sand the rough edges with abrasive paper. Use a cloth to rub shellac into the wood.

3 Screw the pipe holders to the wall. Fix the rail in place. Hang the blankets over the rail, with a 35cm (14in) overlap to make a pelmet, pinning it in place with kilt pins.

CHAIRS AND TABLES

Tables and chairs are two of the most important elements in every home – they appear in most rooms and in many shapes and forms from the elegant and luxurious to the everyday and useful. Everyone needs somewhere to sit and something to eat off! As they usually grace communal spaces such as kitchens or living rooms, they can suffer more than other furniture from day to day living – from busy mealtimes, young children or family pets. They are also relatively quick to show wear and tear and very expensive to replace when they start to look a little ragged round the edges.

If you are short of time and have a limited budget, this chapter will provide simple solutions for instant, affordable and creative table and chair decoration ideas. This thrifty chic is tremendously satisfying. Easy to follow steps demonstrate how to paint, glue, tie, pin and staple a wide variety of materials, providing new looks for old favourites. Each project is self-contained and fully illustrated with clear, step-by-step photographs.

Quite often you will find that furniture needs little more than a new cover or a decorative paint effect to give it a whole new lease of life, so you certainly won't have to think of sacrificing every weekend to take on a project. And by giving a bit of tender, loving care to an old junk-shop find – bought for next-to-nothing and revamped at minimum cost – you can create an individual masterpiece of your own, giving your home a real sense of personal style. Flick through our wonderful and innovative ideas for treatments and simple embellishments, then arm yourself with a paintbrush or a staple gun and have some fun!

Opposite: From the understated elegance of a white dining room to the quirky kitch of a pink bedroom, or the eco-chic of recycled card, there are all sorts of ways to jazz up your favourite old tables and chairs.

DRESSING FOR DINNER

FOR VERY SPECIAL OCCASIONS, why not dress up your table and chairs. Choose a style of corsage suited to the style of your chairs. A simple unvarnished country chair, for instance, calls for understated trimmings, whereas a fancy French one requires something much more elaborate. Trim the table to match. The individual flower arrangements can be given to your guests to take home. These ideas could not be simpler, but will add to the festivities.

YOU WILL NEED

silk or fresh flowers

fresh greenery

florist's wire

scissors

2.5 m (2.5 yd)
organza ribbon

pot-pourri and star anise

glue gun and glue sticks

fine string

beads

A CHAIR WITH STYLE

1 Use florist's wire to join the flowers together at the stem. Silk flowers are best because they bend as you like.

2 Continue binding in flowers and greenery. Trim the stems and tuck in any ends.

3 Finish with a ribbon bow. Make a wire hook to fix the corsage to the chair.

LIVENING UP THE TABLE

1 Fill a teapot with pot-pourri. Then cut a circle from organza, fill it with pot-pourri and tie the top with string. Twist a cinnamon stick into the tie and tie the bag to the lid.

2 Make a necklace for a bottle by pulling apart a piece of fine string into separate strands and glueing star anises to one strand.

3 Decorate a decanter or jar with a piece of organza ribbon tied into bows, or threaded with beads.

PURE PLASTIC

A PLASTIC TABLECLOTH is invaluable on a table that gets a lot of use – in a family breakfast room, for example – as it can be wiped clean in seconds and doesn't stain. As a rule, however, ready-made plastic cloths tend to be very plain or extremely garish. To make an attractive as well as practical cloth, why not cut a shaped trim from plain white plastic and make a simple design along the edge using a hole punch? Inexpensive, quick and very easy to make – what could be better? You could also make a matching cloth for a sideboard or serving area.

YOU WILL NEED

tape measure

plastic fabric

dressmaker's scissors

pencil

cardboard

scissors

hole punch

ribbon, string or rope (optional)

1 Measure your table and cut the plastic fabric to the required size. Draw up and cut out a cardboard template for the scalloped edge. Draw lightly around the template on the wrong side of the plastic fabric with a pencil.

2 Cut the edging shape with sharp dressmaker's scissors, keeping the scallops rounded and even.

3 Punch out a design with a hole punch. You could thread ribbon, string or rope through the holes to add even more interest and, perhaps, a splash of colour.

TACTILE TABLECLOTH

A MASS OF ALL sorts of wonderful trimmings is now available and a trip around the haberdashery (notions) department will, with a little imagination, generate any number of ideas. Here, simple upholsterer's webbing was used to edge a plain and practical hessian (burlap) cloth. The webbing was decorated with string in very loose loops. The charm of this simple design lies in its interesting textures, so it is probably best to use materials in toning colours, as here. However, if you wish, you could make a bold statement in bright primaries or contrasting shades.

YOU WILL NEED

about 2 m (2.5 yd) hessian (burlap)
dressmaker's scissors
dressmaker's pins
needle and tacking thread
iron
sewing machine and
matching sewing thread
8 m (8¾ yd) webbing
brown string

1 Cut the hessian (burlap) to the size you require, allowing for hems. Turn under the hems and pin, tack, press and machine-stitch. Cut a length of webbing to go round all four sides. Pin and machine-stitch the webbing around the edge.

2 Lay the string on the length of webbing and twist it to experiment with different designs – a repeating pattern will look more professional.

3 Pin, tack and hand-stitch the string to the webbing, to hold it securely. It doesn't matter if there are gaps in the stitching; the looseness of the string is all part of the effect.

POLYNESIAN THRONE

A SPLENDID ADDITION to your conservatory or log-cabin-style summer house, this chair festooned with wheat and rushes is not destined to be a mere garden seat, but a haven for sitting and musing. Gardening has become one of the most popular pastimes and garden centres are full of a huge variety of plants and garden paraphernalia. Customized garden furniture is much sought after and pricey, but you can make this stylish throne for very little cost, with dried grasses, craft brushes, raffia and twigs, which are available from garden centres or florists.

YOU WILL NEED

wooden chair

medium-grade abrasive paper

oil-based brown paint

paintbrush

4 large bunches of wheat

large hank of raffia

double-sided tape

craft rush brushes

saw

staple gun

dried bamboo or rushes

1 Sand the wooden surfaces, to provide a key for the paint. Paint the chair with the brown paint to give it a woodgrain effect. You may find it easier to remove the seat.

2 Cover the horizontal strut of the back rest with a few lengths of wheat, tying them in place with raffia. Use the double-sided tape to hold the wheat while you work (the final fixing comes later). Attach two rush brushes diagonally, by binding the stalks to the chair frame and at the crossing point with raffia. Shorten the two remaining rush brushes to the length of the vertical chair struts.

3 To cover the verticals of the back rest, bind them with several strands of raffia. Slot stems of wheat through the raffia until the wood is covered. Tie the shortened brushes to the front horizontals and verticals.

4 Bind the two side brushes with many twinings of raffia. Discreetly part the brushes and secure them at the top with a few strengthening staples. Add decorative and reinforcing raffia in crisscross fashion to the back of the chair. Knot the raffia to secure it.

5 Choose thin, flexible bamboo or rushes to bend over the top of the legs, staple in place then bind with raffia. Staple a rough covering of wheat and rushes over the legs. As a final touch, and to help it last, knot and crisscross more raffia between your turns.

BUCKET STOOL

FLORIST'S BUCKETS in galvanized tin are widely available in a variety of heights – obviously, the taller they are, the better. Cover the metal seat pad in any fabric (a waffle towel was used here). For a bathroom you could fill PVC or clear plastic fabric with foam chips or fun sponges. Tea towels also make fun covers and a layer of dried lavender would make a lovely scented seat.

YOU WILL NEED

1 m (1 yd) heavy cord or rope
2 florist's buckets
glue gun
very large self-cover buttons
scraps of material for
covering buttons
fabric-cutting tool for
buttons
waffle hand towel
circular cushion pad
large sewing needle
matching thread

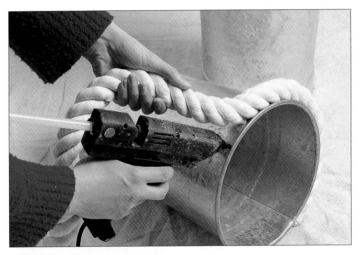

1 Attach the cord or rope to the top rim of one of the buckets with the glue gun.

2 Place this bucket inside the second bucket, applying glue to its rim, then invert both buckets.

3 Use the fabric to cover the buttons, following the manufacturer's instructions. The special tool for cutting the fabric is invaluable for this job.

4 Sew the buttons to the centre of the waffle hand towel. Then use the towel to cover the cushion pad. Instead of smoothing out the gathering in the fabric, accentuate it, using the buttons as a focus. Glue the pad to the upturned bucket.

CARDBOARD CHAIR

IT'S VERY IMPORTANT that you hunt down the correct cardboard of the heaviest weight direct from a cardboard manufacturer for this chair. Here, a substantial "treble-skinned" cardboard has been used. The template shows how to make the chair by judicious folding. Remember that, as with wood, the vertical grain is the strongest. Cardboard furniture is particularly suitable for children, because of their lighter weight. To hold your cardboard creation securely together, use gum arabic tape, as it is a deceptively strong brown parcel tape and therefore perfect for this project.

YOU WILL NEED

felt-tipped pen

metal ruler

4 sheets of treble-skinned cardboard, 2 x 1.5m (2 x 1¹/₂yd)

scissors

craft knife

self-healing cutting mat

gum arabic tape

4 thin dowels, pencils or chopsticks, 13cm (5in)

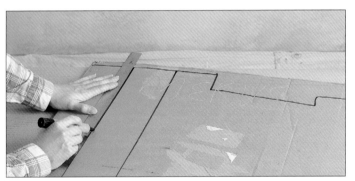

1 Draw the design directly on to the cardboard, using the diagrams on the next page as a guide. Make sure that you keep the grain of the cardboard running from the top of the chair to the bottom.

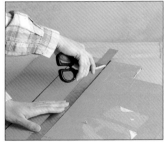

2 Using the back of the scissors and the metal ruler, score along the fold lines and, using a craft knife, cut out all the shapes and bind the edges with gum arabic tape.

3 Assemble the chair in the same way as you would make a carton, folding and slotting the cardboard into itself. The back rest of the chair has flaps that fold into the arm rests.

4 Slot the seat into position, making sure it is securely held in place. To give further support on the struts, peg pieces of dowel, or even pencils or chopsticks, through the cross-struts.

LIGHT AND SHADE

The lighting in any room is crucial as it can have a huge impact on the overall atmosphere. You can use it to highlight the contours of a room, to draw attention to desirable features and to tempt the eye away from less impressive corners.

The options for interesting lights are endless, from high-tech spotlights to traditional standard lamps and classical sconces, and in this chapter we have tried to explore plenty of alternatives. Simple, step-by-step photographs show how to transform everyday lampshades and bases by using interesting paint techniques, by embellishing them with raffia or covering them with beads. You can take a basic frame and cover it with tissue paper, or wrap it with muslin (cheesecloth), or create a table lamp from bamboo – all the projects we have chosen are clearly photographed and provide a stunning gallery of different treatments for painting, adapting and decorating light fittings of all kinds. A good starting point is to look at the lights that are already in your home. Some of the quick projects could be just what is needed to give them an injection of style. Bases and shades can both be transformed with simple paint techniques or bead fringing, or stamped with paper designs. Patterns can be cut out of paper shades, to allow shards of light to escape, and tin shades can be drilled or pierced for a similar effect.

Old-fashioned wall lights that you no longer admire can be replaced with small spotlights and cunningly shaded with unusual objects such as baskets, colanders, roof slates… or perhaps you will come up with an original idea of your own.

Lighting is more than a practical necessity, it is one of the interior designer's most powerful tools, so use it creatively and really enjoy transforming the look of your rooms.

Opposite: Light is the easiest way to transform any environment, from the warm and comforting to the bright and lively. Try changing your current plain shades for one of these new ideas.

BENT-WIRE CHANDELIER

MAGICALLY CRAFTED FROM a roll of wire, this delicate little chandelier was twisted and curled into shape with long-nosed pliers. Making it is so much fun that you will probably want to make a pair. Bonsai-training wire, sold in garden centres and by bonsai-tree specialists, was used here. Hang the chandelier from a chain and hook so that it can twist and turn in passing air currents.

YOU WILL NEED

roll of silver bonsai-training wire

wire cutters

long-nosed pliers

roll of gardening wire

4 self-tapping screws and screwdriver

glue gun with all-purpose glue sticks

4 drawing pins (thumb tacks)

4 night-lights

large sequins

1 Cut a 35cm (13¾in) length of bonsai wire for the first kidney-shaped curl. Hold the wire with one hand, grip the end with the pliers and shape a curl. Holding the first curl in your hand, curl the other end. Make a single curl from a smaller piece of wire.

2 Make two more single curls. Each branch is made of these four pieces. Cut a 12cm (4¾in) length of gardening wire and bind the kidney-shaped curl and two of the single curls together, as shown. Wind the wire round neatly like a spring.

3 Screw a self-tapping screw into the centre of the binding, leaving at least 1cm (½in) protruding at the top.

4 Bind the third single curl on to the back of the kidney shape, winding a length of gardening wire into a neat binding as before. Snip off the end of the gardening wire at an angle, close to the binding. Repeat the above steps to make the four branches.

5 Cut a 50cm (20in) length of bonsai wire for the central column. Twist one end into a spiral and the other into a small hook. Make two small, tight curls and bind them into the top end of the column, facing inwards. Bind the four branches on to the column.

6 Apply a dot of glue to one of the screw heads and immediately sit a drawing pin (thumb tack) on it, point upwards. Repeat with the remaining screw heads. Press a night-light down on to each of the drawing pins. Thread the large sequins on to the curls.

ANGULAR UPLIGHTER

THIS UNUSUAL WALL LIGHT IS a two-coloured plastic shade slotted over a standard mini-spotlight. The two halves of the shade are simply clamped together with two shiny sprung paper clips on each side. Before fitting the two pieces together, cut a hole in the back piece to slot over the base of the spotlight. Make the hole the same size as the spotlight base so that it fits snugly and will not slip. Fit the back of the shade in position first, making sure that the bulb will remain well clear of the plastic to avoid damage to the shade and any potential accidents.

YOU WILL NEED

brown wrapping paper

pencil

ruler and set square

scissors

spray adhesive

sheet of yellow plastic

sheet of red plastic

craft knife and cutting mat

small halogen wall-light fixture

4 small sprung paper clips

1 Enlarge the template on a photocopier. Transfer it twice to brown wrapping paper. Cut out the two patterns, leaving a 2cm (³⁄₄in) seam allowance all around the edges.

2 Spray the paper patterns with adhesive and stick one on each plastic sheet. Cut out the shapes and nick the ends of the fold lines, so that they will be obvious from both sides.

3 Remove the paper, then score the fold line, but do not cut more than the surface as you do it. Practise on the off-cuts first to get the pressure right.

4 Turn the sheets over and score the fold lines again, working between the nicks at each end. Fold up the shades. Cut a hole in the back shade to fit the spotlight base, place it over the spotlight, then attach the front piece with paper clips.

PINK TISSUE SHADE

THIS BRILLIANT PINK PAPER lampshade will make a stunning centrepiece for a room and will cast a flattering pink light over everything – and everyone – at the same time. Make the size of the lampshade appropriate for your room. As it is very lightweight, it can be made quite big, which is useful if your house has high ceilings. Attach equal lengths of chain to the curled hooks and hang the light fitting in the centre, so that the hot air rises out of the top of the shade.

YOU WILL NEED

bonsai-training wire

wire cutters

thinner wire

long-nosed pliers

chains to hang the shade

glue gun with all-purpose glue sticks

bright pink, good-quality tissue paper

water-based varnish

paintbrush

1 Cut three equal lengths of bonsai wire for the struts. Bend them into wavy shapes. You can exaggerate the shape as the wire will spring back a little. Bind the ends together with thinner wire, using long-nosed pliers.

2 Attach a length of the thinner wire about 12 cm (4¾in) from the end of one strut, winding it around to secure it. Then take it around the other two struts in the same way. This will form the top of the framework. Wind around two more lengths of the thinner wire in the same way.

3 Using the pliers, curl the ends of the struts where the chains will be attached. Apply glue to one of the struts and fold the edge of a piece of tissue paper over it. Stretch the tissue across and glue it to the next strut.

4 Continue in this way, overlapping where necessary, until the framework is covered. Wind and glue a strip around the point where the three struts are joined. Brush on a coat of varnish to tighten up the paper and bond the layers.

ECCENTRIC CREPE

CREPE BANDAGE IS GREAT material to work with and makes a fun lampshade. It has just enough stretch to give a good tight fit and the textured surface clings to itself as you layer the bandage. Keep an even tension as you wind it around a wire frame and use hot glue at key points, if necessary, to prevent any slipping or sagging. Make sure you leave an opening at the top, however, to allow the hot air to escape.

YOU WILL NEED

copper bonsai-training wire

wire cutters

long-nosed pliers

thinner wire

glue gun with all-purpose glue sticks

rolls of bandage

1 Cut three equal lengths of bonsai training wire and bend each one into three curves, using the pliers. The wire will straighten up when you release it, so exaggerate the shapes as you bend them.

2 Bind the three ends of the bonsai wire firmly together with the thinner wire. Be generous with the amount of wire because you need to make a solid fixture. Use the long-nosed pliers to help you to bind tightly.

3 Run another length of wire between the three struts, winding it tightly around each strut, to form the lowest of three enclosing wires that will later provide the framework for the bandage binding.

4 Wind round two more lengths of wire to complete the frame. Twist the ends of the struts into curved "feet".

5 Glue the bandage to a strut about 5cm (2in) from the binding at the top. Wrap tightly to fix firmly. Wrap the bandage around the framework, pulling it to get the tension right. Apply glue whenever it crosses a strut.

6 Wrap and glue a small length of bandage to cover the wire binding right at the top of the framework. Use the glue gun to seal the edge and be sure to leave a 5cm (2in) gap around the top in order for the heat to escape.

TRIMMED SHADE

TURN A RATHER BORING, plain-coloured lampshade into a completely wacky extrovert by adding a dangling fringe of unusual trimmings. Almost anything non-perishable that will thread can be used – the brighter it is, the better. The choice is yours. For ideas, check out the toy store, especially the pocket money selection, where bright beads, miniature dolls and animals and fluorescent plastic balls are all waiting to be snapped up. Another good source of trimmings is the stationery store; multicoloured plastic paper clips and even treasury tags can be put to a decorative use their inventors would never have credited.

YOU WILL NEED

plain conical lampshade

square of paper or cardboard

pencil

set square

hole punch

strong thread

needle

selection of beads, toys, baubles, etc.

glue (optional)

1 Place the lampshade on a square of paper or cardboard and draw around the bottom edge in pencil.

2 Use a set square to divide the circle into eight equal segments.

3 Replace the shade on the paper or cardboard and mark the divisions around the edge in pencil.

4 Use the hole punch to make eight small holes about 1cm (¹/₂in) up from the edge of the shade, in line with the pencil marks.

5 Attach a bead securely at the end of the length of thread, as an anchor, then thread on a selection of your chosen baubles and beads.

6 Fix to the shade by sewing the thread through one of the punched holes several times, finishing with a secure knot. An extra bead can be glued to the edge of the shade to cover the thread. Decorate the rest of the shade in the same way.

TRIO OF LAMPSHADES

NOTHING COULD BE QUICKER, easier or cheaper than painting squiggles, spots or flecks of colour on a few plain lampshades to add a touch of individuality to any room. The three shades shown here have each been made using a different decorative technique. All are fun to do, and only the black-and-white stripes require a steady hand. Use plain fabric shades and experiment with colour, using it to reinforce an existing decorating theme or to add a spark of brilliance and give a quick face-lift to a monotonous colour scheme.

YOU WILL NEED

BLOTTING-PAPER EFFECT
plain fabric lampshade
paintbrushes
bright blue ready-mixed
watercolour paint
droppered bottle

PAINTED-LINE EFFECT
cardboard
cutting mat
plain fabric lampshade
scalpel
metal ruler
black acrylic paint
paintbrushes: large
square-tipped and small

FLECKED EFFECT
plain fabric lampshade
cardboard
pencil
scalpel
cutting mat
toothbrush
water-based acrylic, poster,
watercolour or gouache
paints: yellow ochre,
brick-red and cream
paintbrush

BLOTTING-PAPER EFFECT

1 Dampen the whole outer surface of the fabric lampshade with water, using a paintbrush.

2 Fill the droppered bottle with blue paint and squeeze it gently to deposit one small drop on to the shade. Watch the blot spread so that you can judge where to position the next drop.

3 Turn the lampshade with your free hand and, as you do so, drop equal amounts of paint, spaced fairly evenly all around the shade.

4 Fill the spaces between the blots with a more random pattern of differently sized dots, but be careful not to cover all the original lampshade colour completely.

5 Holding the lampshade from the inside with your free hand and resting your painting hand on the work surface, paint the top and bottom rims solid blue.

PAINTED-LINE EFFECT

1 Cut a right-angled piece of cardboard with one edge the same length as the height of the shade. Angle the other side to make it easy to hold.

2 Hold the square-edged cardboard up against the shade and paint a wide squiggle to the right of it, using the large brush. After each squiggle, move the cardboard along; this will ensure that you paint vertically and don't slide off in one direction, which is very easily done when painting a shape like this.

3 Paint fine squiggly lines between the fatter ones, using the small paintbrush. Support the wrist of your painting hand with your free hand to keep it steady.

4 Finish off the lampshade by painting the top and bottom rims with a solid black line. ➤

FLECKED EFFECT

1 Place the shade upside down on the piece of cardboard and draw around the inside of the top rim. Cut this circle out, just slightly larger than the drawn pencil line, and place it on top of the shade to prevent any paint from dripping on to the inside.

2 Place the shade on a protected work surface. Fill the toothbrush with the yellow ochre paint, then draw your thumb backwards over the bristles to fleck the lampshade with colour. Try and get a fine, even covering, but allow the background to show through.

3 Clean the toothbrush, then dip it into the brick-red paint. Use the brush at an angle, to make randomly placed wedge-shaped marks at different angles over the flecked pattern. Don't try for a regular pattern: look at the example shown here to judge the effect you are after.

4 To finish the decoration, clean the toothbrush, then apply the cream paint in the same way as the red. It may not show up much but when the lamp is lit at night, all will be revealed.

GILDED PAPER PATCHWORK

GIVE TWO PLAIN LAMPSHADES a glittering new look by covering them in paper patchwork in two different styles. Although the techniques for each shade differ slightly, they have enough in common to be used as a stunning pair. The paper can be any type that is not too thick: newsprint, tissue paper, parcel wrap, photocopied typescript, sheet music or fine woven papers. Make a feature of ragged edges and avoid a regular, neat finish. The very special linking finishing touch is added with flashes of brilliant gold. The leaf used here is called Dutch metal. It is applied in the same way as gold leaf but costs much less. If you have never done gilding before, these shades are a good starting point.

CUT-PAPER PATCHWORK

1 Cut out "squares" from the different materials. Make them roughly equally sized, but trim them at an angle on both sides to taper slightly to fit the shade's conical shape.

2 Try out various combinations of texture and colour until you are happy with the arrangement. Apply wallpaper paste or PVA (white) glue to the backs of the shapes and stick them in place on the shade. Butt them against each other to form a solid patchwork.

3 Paint "stitches" of gold size to link the squares together. Think of patchwork stitching, and make the lines vertical on the top and bottom and horizontal on the sides.

4 Cut the Dutch metal leaf into strips, still on the backing sheet. Gently press the leaf on to the tacky gold size.

5 Use a firm-bristled brush to clean away all the excess leaf, leaving just the stitches. Burnish with a soft cloth.

TORN-PAPER PATCHWORK

1 Tear the different papers into similarly sized shapes, leaving the edges ragged and uneven.

2 Tint one-third of the shapes with shellac. It is fast-drying and will make the papers stiffer and also slightly transparent. Clean the brush with methylated spirits (methyl alcohol).

3 Tint another third of the paper shapes using water-based stain and leave them to dry.

4 Arrange the shapes on the shade, overlapping them in places and making a feature of the ragged edges. Practise with different arrangements until you are happy with the result.

5 Apply wallpaper paste or PVA (white) glue to the backs of the shapes and stick on to the shade, using the stained shapes first. Space wide apart to start and build up gradually.

6 Fill in the gaps with the untinted torn papers.

➤

7 Paint a neat 1 cm (¹/₂in) border line all around the top and bottom of the lampshade with gold size.

8 Cut the sheets of Dutch metal leaf into strips, leaving the backing sheet still in place.

9 Press the strips against the tacky gold size along both edges. Overlap them when you need to; the leaf will only stick to the sized sections.

10 Finally, rub off any excess metal leaf and burnish the entire design to a shine with a soft cloth.

WOODY NIGHTSHADE

WOOD VENEER IS A THIN SHEET shaved from a seasoned tree trunk and is sold by timber merchants who supply furniture makers. Each sheet is unique, so choose the veneer with the best grain; it will look even better with light shining through it. The lampshade shown here is made from flamed-ash veneer. The veneer hangs from a simple wooden frame but you could use a square picture frame (without the glass). Carefully remove one edge of the frame, thread on the curtain (drape) rings and glue the piece back. Suspend the veneer from the frame using clipped curtain rings. Hang the lampshade on leather thongs or cord from a ceiling hook, with a pendant lamp fitting and bulb dangling inside it.

YOU WILL NEED

4 equal lengths of wooden dowel, mitred

glue gun with all-purpose glue sticks

curtain (drape) rings with clip attachments

metal ruler

scalpel

sheet of wood veneer

4 equal lengths of cord or leather thongs

1 Join three pieces of dowel using the glue gun. Thread the rings on to the frame before glueing the last piece of dowel in place.

2 Measure the width of one side of the frame and, using the scalpel, cut four strips of veneer, one for each side. Make the length roughly twice the width; for a natural look the pieces should not be precisely the same size.

3 To finish, attach two clips to each sheet of veneer, then tie a cord or thong to each corner for hanging.

CONTAINERS

CONTAINER DECORATING PROVIDES imaginative and innovative projects for transforming old containers or creating new ones in quick, simple, stylish and beautiful ways. Put an end to cluttered shelves and overcrowded wardrobes, protect your belongings from dust, spillages or breakages and find exciting ways to jazz up your home.

If you've always thought of containers as mere practical objects in which to store anything from flowers to cookies, then you will be amazed at how cheap, everyday items can be easily made over into chic containers, bringing a personal dash of style into every room in your house. Take old paint tins, jam jars, bottles, bags, baskets or shoe boxes and give them a whole new lease of life by converting them into plant pots, shoe racks or funky chests of drawers – cover them with fabric, perhaps, or glue on buttons, beads or shells… there are no limits to what you can do. The projects we show you can serve as a source of ideas to help you add a variety of colours, textures, patterns and shapes to whatever style of organization you opt for. Whichever project you choose to make, you can simply use our suggestions as a springboard for your own creativity, so don't be afraid to amend or embellish once your confidence has grown. Adapt ideas and techniques to suit your own style and existing decor.

An afternoon spent sticking and gluing is totally absorbing and at the end of the day you will have a wonderful sense of achievement, too. All the techniques used here are clearly photographed for each project and are designed to be easy to follow. Throw inhibition to the wind and enjoy creating great-looking effects at next to no cost!

Opposite: From laundry to bric-a-brac, everything has to have a place, so make yours funky or rustic to suit your mood and your interior.

STRING BOTTLES

LIQUEUR BOTTLES HAVE SUCH lovely shapes that it seems a shame to put them into the recycling bin. This method of recycling enables you to keep on enjoying them even after you have enjoyed their contents! The bottles used here are sherry, crème de menthe and Armagnac. This project is very easy to do and it can almost seem like therapy once you've gathered together a ball of string, some glue, a pair of scissors and three interestingly shaped bottles. Make yourself comfortable, put on some relaxing music and start winding the string round the bottles.

YOU WILL NEED

ball of string

glue gun with all-purpose glue sticks (or all-purpose glue)

3 interestingly shaped bottles

scissors

1 Coil one end of the string round like a drinks mat to make a base. Place a dot of glue in the centre of the bottle base. Heat the glue gun and apply glue in spokes over the base. Press the string on to them. Draw a ring of glue round the edge to make the base secure.

2 Circle the bottle with the string, working your way up and applying sufficient glue as you go. Make sure you get a good bonding on the bends and curves.

3 When you reach the top of the bottle, cut the end of the string and apply plenty of glue to it so the finish is neat with no fraying. Repeat these steps with the other bottles.

FANCIFUL SHOE BOX

IF YOU ARE ONE of those people who always takes the shoe box home with new shoes, only to throw it away reluctantly a while later, then this is the project for you! Your instincts to take the box in the first place are right, as shoe boxes are the perfect shape and size to make useful containers. This box was covered with brown wrapping paper – yet more good recycling – that was rolled and twisted, then unravelled and stuck on to the box to provide an interesting textured surface. The "bark" is made from torn strips of white paper, coated with wood stain to give a streaky finish. The end result is a unique, natural-looking container suitable for anything from pot-pourri to a card index system.

YOU WILL NEED

shoe box

cream emulsion (latex) paint

paintbrushes

brown wrapping paper

pre-mixed wallpaper paste, and cheap brush

scissors

PVA (white) glue

thick white paper

wood stain (such as antique pine)

thick, coarse string

piece of calico, 10 x 10cm (4 x 4in)

bulldog clips

glue gun with all-purpose glue sticks (or all-purpose glue)

1 Paint the shoe box with cream paint until all of the lettering is completely covered. Leave to dry.

2 Roll up some wrapping paper, crumpling it. Fold up, twisting as small as possible. Untwist and open out.

3 Apply a coat of wallpaper paste to the box. Place it centrally on the parcel wrap.

4 Fold the wrapping paper round the box, pressing it into the pasted surface, but not smoothing it too much. Pinch the paper along the edges of the box and cut along these. Fold the end flaps inside, sticking them with wallpaper paste.

5 Fold the wrapping paper round the sides of the box, one end at a time, pasting one on top of the other to create two large triangular shapes.

6 Fold the triangular shapes up over the sides and paste them against the inside of the box.

7 Neaten the inside by cutting a piece of wrapping paper to fit the base. Paste it over the paper edges.

8 Using a dry brush, paint a streaky coat of undiluted PVA (white) glue on the white paper. Leave some areas of the paper unpainted, to allow the wood stain to show through. Leave to dry completely.

9 Brush wood stain on to the white paper. It will be resisted by the PVA glue where it is at its thickest and part-resisted in other places. This gives the bark effect.

10 Tear the paper into rough triangular shapes. If you tear at a slight angle, the paper will rip through its thickness and make the edges white and thin. Paint these white edges with wood stain so that they blend in. ➤

11 Roll up the paper triangles, beginning with the widest part and rolling towards the point. Bundle the strips together with string and tie a reef knot. Separate the strands of string so that they bush out from the knot.

12 Fray the edges of the calico piece, then scrunch it up in the middle, using clips to hold the shape. Heat the glue gun and apply glue to the scrunched folds. Press the calico on to the centre of the box lid.

13 Remove the clips from the calico and apply more hot glue. Press the bark bundle on top of the calico.

14 If you are using the box to store a card index, write labelling on some spare "bark" paper and glue this to one end of the box.

STAR CUPBOARD

THIS ATTRACTIVE LITTLE cupboard fits in anywhere the moment you have finished it. While its style is individual, it is also understated, with that comfortable, lived-in look. It was painted, stamped, then painted again and finally it was given a coat of antiquing varnish and rubbed back with a cloth in places. It glows from all the attention and took just one afternoon to make. This style of decoration is so simple that you might consider transforming other furniture in the same way.

YOU WILL NEED

wooden cupboard

emulsion (latex) paint (olive-green, off-white and vermilion)

paintbrushes

scalpel

kitchen sponge

PVA (white) glue

matt varnish (antique pine)

kitchen cloth

1 Paint the cupboard with a coat of olive-green paint. While the paint is drying, use the scalpel to cut the foam into a star shape.

2 Pour some off-white paint on to a plate. Dip a sponge star into the paint and print stars all over the cupboard. Leave to dry.

3 Make a mixture of two-thirds vermilion paint and one-third PVA (white) glue and coat the cupboard.

4 Finish with a coat of tinted varnish, then use a cloth to rub some off each of the stars.

LIZARD-SKIN BOXES

THESE SMART ANGULAR BOXES look crisp and exclusive, but they are, in fact, no more than paper-covered foam board! They make great containers for jewellery, hair-slides or cufflinks and they would add a touch of elegance to any desk or dressing-table. When you make your own boxes, there are no manufacturing constraints, so you can make them any shape you like, however unconventional. Foam board is light and easy to cut and stick. Buy it from art and craft suppliers, and buy lizard-skin paper from specialist paper shops.

YOU WILL NEED

foam board

cutting board

felt-tipped marker pen

ruler

craft knife

glue gun with all-purpose glue sticks (or all-purpose glue)

3 different lizard-skin papers

1 spray adhesive

1 Place the foam board on a cutting board and mark a four-sided angular shape for the base. Cut out the shape. Measure each side, then decide on the height of your box. Cut out four rectangular side sections to fit those measurements. Heat the glue gun and run a thin strip of glue along each base edge, then stick the sides on. The glue will set straight away, so work quickly and accurately.

2 Place the box on a sheet of foam board and draw round it. Add 3–4cm (1¼–1½in) all round for the lid overlap. Cut this out. Do this again, taking off 1 cm (½in) all round, for the lower half of the lid. Glue the two lid sections together. Cut a strip of lizard-skin paper wide enough to line the inside and outside of the box and to fold underneath. Apply spray adhesive to the paper, then wrap it round the box.

3 Cut down into the corners and fold the paper inside the box. Do the same underneath, smoothing the paper flat on to the box. Apply more glue where necessary.

4 Cut out paper for the lid. Glue in place and cut corners. Cut two identical shapes for a handle and glue together. Cover the handle with paper and glue to the top of the box.

ALL BOXED UP

THERE IS A HUGE VARIETY of boxes available, ranging from plain and simple white wooden boxes via shoe boxes to oval trinket boxes. Make a toning set of three using easily available natural materials. However, boxes can be trimmed with almost anything you like: bottletops, paper clips, string, rope or a collage of stamps. Linen tape (used in upholstery or for tags) is available from haberdashery (notions) departments.

1 Measure the plain wooden box. Allow an extra 2cm (¾in) at one end for the toggle and about 7.5cm (3in) for the loop and tag. Cut two lengths of linen tape to this length. Sew a loop in the end of each tape and attach the wooden beads to be used as toggles.

2 Secure the tape to one end of the box with glue, leaving the toggle and loop free so the lid can be opened. Repeat on the other side. Glue a larch twig to the top of the lid, as a decorative "handle".

3 For the slatted wooden box, sort through the pot-pourri and choose the items you would like to use. Glue them to the lid. Glue the dried leaves and cones to the Shaker box, and glue linen tape around the sides.

ORIGAMI BOXES

ORIGAMI IS THE JAPANESE ART of paper-folding, where the most extraordinary three-dimensional objects are made from a single folded square of paper. This little box is a suitable project for a beginner, but it may take a couple of practice attempts before it suddenly "clicks". You can make the boxes any size you like, and use any paper that is not too flimsy. Brown wrapping paper is good as it creases well and is cheap and strong.

YOU WILL NEED

sheet of paper

scissors

double-sided tape
(this breaks all the rules!)

selection of paper squares
for practice (optional)

1 Fold and trim a sheet of paper to make a perfect square. Fold the square corner to corner. Open it to show the creases of four equal triangles. Turn it over and fold into four square quarters. Unfold it so you can see the creases of eight equal triangles. The centre of the paper is Point A.

2 Hold the model in the air and push all the sides together so that the corners meet in the middle. Flatten the model. Point A is now a corner of the flattened model. Keep it facing you.

3 Fold the point opposite Point A over to meet it. Crease it along the mid-line. Now fold it back up to the mid-line and crease the fold. Unfold it again. Fold the same point up to the last crease, then fold it over again, up to the mid-line. Turn the model over and repeat this step.

4 With point A still facing you, take the top layer of the left-hand corner and fold it over on to the right-hand corner. You are now faced with a square. Fold the left-hand corner and the top layer of the right-hand corner into the centre point, and crease. Bring the right-hand top layer over on to the left. Turn over and repeat.

5 Point A now forms the base of a smaller triangle. Fold this up at the point where it meets the sides. Crease, fold it in the other direction and crease. Unfold. Insert your hand and splay your fingers while pushing up the bottom of the model, Point A. Fold down the two pointed sides level with the others and tuck the ends under. Secure with a small piece of tape.

ALL THE TRIMMINGS

CHOOSE THE CHEERFUL PRIMARY colours of blue and red and team them with white for a crisp, clean look with a slightly nautical feel. Equally, you can trim black with white for classic appeal or use toning colours for adding a subtle lift. Felt is an easy, lovely and inexpensive way to trim plain fabrics, whether on shoe bags, linen bags, throws or cushions. You can add as much or as little decoration as you choose.

YOU WILL NEED

round template

2 squares of red felt,
about 20 x 20cm (8 x 8in)

2 squares of blue felt,
about 20 x 20cm (8 x 8in)

dressmaker's pins

fabric marker

pinking shears

blue cord

string

needle

matching sewing thread

fabric item, such as a
shoe bag or quilt

1 Find a round template: it could be a tin lid, coin or anything similar. Place the template on the felt, and draw round the template with a fabric marker. Cut around the circle with pinking shears.

2 Pin two circles together, knot short lengths of cord and sew them on to the circles.

3 Repeat with lengths of string. Sew the circles on to your shoe bag, quilt or other fabric items.

NEWS ON SHOES

SPECIAL SHOES DESERVE a home of their own and these sturdy wooden wine boxes can be made stylish enough to house anything from country brogues to Cinderella's glass slippers. The boxes were lined with different types of newsprint, which was layered and stuck down like papier mâché. Select your newsprint to suit your shoes – put leather lace-ups in the pink financial pages, party shoes in comic strips and velvet pumps in the arts and literary review pages.

YOU WILL NEED

wooden wine crates

abrasive paper

PVA (white) glue

paintbrushes

variety of newsprint

craft knife

clear matt varnish
(or shellac button polish)

1 Sand down the wine crate. Then mix PVA (white) glue with water (50:50) and apply a coat to the inside.

2 Apply another coat of the diluted PVA, then smooth newsprint over the inside. Apply undiluted PVA along the top edges and smooth the paper over it. Leave to dry before applying more paper and glue at random.

3 Leave to dry, then trim the paper along the outside top edges with a craft knife. Varnish the whole box with either clear matt varnish or, if you want an "aged" look, shellac. Leave to dry, then re-coat at least twice.

GILDED BOXES

THERE IS NO PAINT OR SPRAY that gives a finish to compare with gold leaf, or its cheaper counterpart, Dutch metal leaf. It glows and glitters and can be burnished with a soft cloth to leave a gleaming surface. The art of gilding is surrounded by mystique because it requires a great deal of skill to lay the fragile sheets of gold leaf on to gold size or glue. This design was created using a kit suitable for beginners, which can be bought from art and craft suppliers. The flat surface of the box makes it easy to apply, but it is important to follow the manufacturer's instructions as the drying time is crucial to the success of the project.

YOU WILL NEED

design tracing or photocopy

spray adhesive

high-density foam

craft knife

round painted wooden box
with lid

fine-grade abrasive paper

pencil

gold leaf kit

paintbrush

plate

small foam roller

cotton wadding

fine wire wool (optional)

1 Select a suitable design or motif from a source book, and photocopy or trace to size. Spray the back of the design with adhesive and stick it on to a block of foam.

2 Carefully cut out the design, starting in the middle. Then cut around the outside.

3 Once the cutting is complete, carefully peel off the paper pattern.

4 Rub the entire surface of the painted box lightly with fine-grade abrasive paper to make a rough surface for applying the gold size.

5 Draw a pencil line around the top edge of the lid. Use your fingers to keep the line an even distance from the edge.

6 Carefully paint a strip of gold size between the edge of the box lid and the pencil line.

7 Put some size on to a plate and run the roller through it until it is evenly coated. Using the roller, coat the foam stamp thoroughly and evenly.

8 Stamp an even pattern round the side of the box, re-coating the stamp after each print. Stamp four shapes inside the lid border line and one in the centre.

9 Leave the size until it has the right degree of "tack" (according to the manufacturer's instructions), then invert the lid on to a sheet of gold leaf. Smooth the gold leaf over the edges so that it is in contact with all of the size.

10 Holding the box at an angle, apply the sheets of gold leaf round the sides in the same way. ➤

11 Rub the surface with cotton wadding. All the "un-sized" gold will flake off, leaving the design behind.

12 If the brand new gleaming design overwhelms you, rub the box lightly with wire wool to create an antiqued look.

PUNCHED METAL BUCKET

THE IDEA OF DECORATING metal objects with raised punched patterns has been around ever since sheet metal was invented about 300 years ago. Silver is probably best-known for this decorative treatment, but cheaper metals can also look very impressive. Bare metal buckets are ideal for this sort of pattern-making, and all you need is a pen to draw your guidelines and a hammer and blunt nail for the punching. You can practise your technique on any can to find the ideal sort of tap needed to make a good bump without piercing the metal.

YOU WILL NEED

bare metal bucket

felt-tipped marker pen
(not water-based)

blunt nail
(or centre punch)

hammer

rag

lighter fuel
(or similar solvent)

1 Draw your pattern on the inside of the bucket. These motifs come from South America, but any repeated curves or angles are suitable.

2 Rest the bucket on a piece of wood to protect your work surface. Tap the nail with a hammer, keeping the dents regularly spaced. About 1cm (½in) is fine.

3 Continue hammering the pattern all over the inside of the metal bucket.

4 Use a rag and lighter fuel to clean off the marker pen pattern that is left between the punched marks.

CIRCULAR PAINTED BOXES

THIS PROJECT EXPERIMENTS with three different paint effects. The first, rust, looks especially good when used on a material that doesn't naturally rust, such as wood. Verdigris is a natural substance that forms on the surface of weathered brass and is a beautiful turquoise-green colour. The third finish used here is crackle glaze (craquelure) which looks a bit like lizard skin. This is the most time-consuming of the three paint effects because of the drying time needed between coats.

YOU WILL NEED

3 wooden boxes, with lids

water-based paints: dark grey,
2 shades of rust, green-grey, stone,
2 shades of green and maize yellow
(according to required finish)

handful of fine sand

plate

paintbrushes

3 foam sponges

clear matt varnish,
craquelure base varnish,
craquelure varnish

alizarin crimson oil paint

2 rags

white spirit (paint thinner)

THE RUST FINISH

1 Mix sand into the dark grey base coat for texture. Apply two coats of paint to the box. Leave to dry. Dab on the darker rust colour with a sponge. Cover most of the background.

2 Dab on the lighter rust colour. If you are in any doubt about how it should look, find some real rust and copy it. Finally dab in just a touch of green-grey. Do not overdo this as it should blend in rather than stand out as a sharp contrast.

THE VERDIGRIS FINISH

Paint the box with the stone base coat colour. Dab on the lighter green with a sponge. Cover most of the background with this. Dab on the other green using a sponge. Apply a coat of clear matt varnish to protect the surface.

THE CRACKLE GLAZE FINISH

Paint a yellow base coat and a coat of craquelure base varnish. When dry, apply a coat of craquelure varnish. Leave to dry. Rub crimson oil paint into cracks with a rag. Dip a rag in white spirit (paint thinner); rub the surface so red paint stays in the cracks.

SUPPLIERS AND USEFUL ADDRESSES

UNITED KINGDOM

Axminster Power Tool Centre
Chard Street
Axminster
Devon EX13 5HU
Tel: 01297 33656
Power tools supplier

Black and Decker and Dewalt
210 Bath Road
Slough
Berkshire SL1 3YD
Tel: 01753 567055
Power tools supplier

Colour Centre
Offord Road
London N1
Tel: 020 7609 116
Paints and do-it-yourself
equipment supplier

Foxell and James
Farringdon Road
London EC1M 3JB
Tel: 020 7405 0152
Wax, oil, varnish and finishing
products supplier

Heward and Dean
Grove Park Road
London N15 4SP
Tel: 020 8800 3447
Tools supplier

HSS Power Tools
25 Willow Lane
Mitcham
Surrey CR4 4TS
Tel: 020 8260 3100

James Latham
Leeside Wharf
Mount Pleasant Hill
Clapton E5
Tel: 020 8806 3333
Timber supplier

Plasplugs Ltd.
Wetmore Road
Burton-on-Trent
Staffordshire DE14 1SD
Tel: 01283 530303
www.plasplugs.com
Tiling tools, fixings and
fasteners supplier

Record Tools Ltd.
Parkway Works
Kettlebridge Road
Sheffield S9 3BL
Tel: 0114 244 9066
Hand tools supplier

Ronseal Limited
Thorncliffe Park
Chapeltown
Sheffield S35 2YP
Tel: 0114 246 7171
www.ronseal.co.uk
Ronseal, Colron, Thompson's
products

Spear & Jackson
Neill Tools Ltd.
Atlas Way
Atlas North
Sheffield S4 7QQ
Tel: 0114 261 4242
Tools supplier

Stanley Tools UK Ltd.
Beighton Road East
Drakehouse
Sheffield S20 7JZ
Tel: 0114 276 8888
Tools supplier

Vitrex Ltd.
Everest Road
Lytham St. Annes
Lancashire
FY8 3AZ
Tel: 01253 789180
Tools and clothing supplier

Woodfit Ltd.
Kem Mill
Whittle-le-Woods
Chorley
Lancashire PR6 7EA
Tel: 01257 266421
Furniture fittings supplier

UNITED STATES

**Compton Lumber &
Hardware Inc.**
P.O. Box 84972
Seattle, WA 98124-6272
Tel: (206) 623-5010
www.comptonlbr.com

Constantine's
2050 Eastchester Road
Bronx, New York
NY 10461
Tel: (718) 792-1600
www.constantines.com

The Cutting Edge, Inc.
7123 Southwest Freeway
Houston,
TX 77074
Tel: (981) 9228
www.cuttingedgetools.com

Northern Tool and Equipment
Corporate Headquarters
2800 Southcross Drive West
Burnsville, MN 55306
Tel: (800) 533-5545
www.northerntool.com

AUSTRALIA

BBC Hardware Stores
Hardware House
For details of your nearest store
in either of the above two
chains, contact (02) 9876 0888.

Mitre 10
For details of your nearest store
contact (03) 9703 4200.

Bunnings Warehouse
For details of your nearest store
contact (03) 9607 0777.

Thrifty-Link Hardware
See you local state directory for
your nearest store.

USEFUL ADDRESSES

British Cement Association
Century House
Telford Avenue
Berkshire RG45 6YS
Tel: 01344 762676
www.bca.org.uk

**British Wood Preserving and
Damp-proofing Association**
1 Gleneagles House
Vernon Gate, South Street
Derby DE1 1UP
Tel: 01332 225100
www.bwpda.co.uk

**Conservatory Association/
Glass and Glazing Federation**
44–48 Borough High Street
London SE1 1XB
Tel: 01480 458278
www.ggf.org.uk

Energy Saving Trust
21 Dartmouth Street
London SW1H 9BT
Tel: 08457 277200
www.est.org.uk

**Home Energy Efficiency
Scheme**
Eaga Partnership
2nd Floor, Eldon Court
Eldon Square
Newcastle-upon-Tyne
NE1 7HA
Tel: 0800 316 6011

Kitchen Specialists Association
12 Top Barn Business Centre
Holt Heath
Worcester WR6 6NH
Tel: 01905 726066
www.ksa.co.uk

**Laminated Glass
Information Centre**
299 Oxford Street
London W1R 1LA
020 7499 1720
www.martex.co.uk/prca/condor

**National Association of Loft
Insulation Contractors
and
National Cavity Insulation
Association**
PO Box 12
Hazlemere
Surrey GU27 3AH
Tel: 01428 654011
theceed@computer.com

National Fireplace Association
6th Floor
The McLaren Building
35 Dale End
Birmingham B4 7LN
Tel: 0121 200 1310

**RIBA (Royal Institute of
Chartered Architects)**
66 Portland Place
London W1B 1AD
Tel: 020 7580 5533
www.architecture.com

SALVO
(Directory of Salvage Yards)
PO Box 333
Cornhill on Tweed
Northumberland TD12 4YJ
Tel: 01890 820333
www.salvo.co.uk

**The Association of Noise
Consultants**
6 Trap Road
Guilden Morden
Hertfordshire SG8 0JE
Tel: 01763 852958
www.association-of-noise-
consultants.co.uk

**The Institute of Electrical
Engineers**
2 Savoy Place
London WC2R 0BL
Tel: 020 7240 1871
www.iee.org.uk

The Institute of Plumbing
64 Station Lane
Hornchurch
Essex RM12 6NB
Tel: 01708 472791
www.plumbers.org.uk

GLOSSARY

Architrave (trim) A type of timber moulding, used mainly around openings in walls for doors.

Batten (furring strip) A straight length of timber, used for temporary or permanent support, e.g. of roof tiles, wall tiles or for setting concrete.

Bevel An angled edge on, for example, a piece of wood. Also see chamfer. Also a carpenter's tool for setting an angle.

Bolster (stonecutter's) chisel A flat-bladed chisel used for cutting masonry. Used widely by electricians, plumbers and paving contractors; can also be used for levering up floorboards.

Building regulations Legal requirements in the UK and other countries for the ways that houses are constructed (and modified).

Butt joint A joint between two pieces of timber when one piece simply meets the other, such as in an L-shape or a T-shape or end-to-end.

Casement window A window (or light), which is hinged at one side or at the top.

Caulking gun A device for squeezing sealant or adhesive out of a cartridge.

Cavity wall A method of house construction, where the outer walls of the house consist of two "leaves" (typically one of brick and one of lightweight block) with a gap (cavity) between them.

Centre point The sharp point of a twist drill bit or a metal plug put into a dowel hole to transfer its position to a second piece of wood.

Chamfer An angled edge to timber, usually smaller than a bevel.

Chipboard (particle board) An inexpensive manufactured board consisting of timber scraps and glue.

Clearance hole A hole drilled to take the full size of a screw.

Consumer unit The modern term for an electrical fuse-box. It may contain miniature

circuit breakers rather than fuses depending on its age.

Combination ladder A ladder that can be used in two or more ways. Uses include: step-ladder, straight ladder, stair ladder and extending ladder.

Cornice, Cove (crown molding) A decorative timber, plaster or polystyrene (styrofoam) moulding to cover up the join between wall and ceiling.

Counterbore To enlarge a hole, for example to take a bolt or screw head.

Countersink An angled recess to take the head of a countersunk screw. Also tool for making the same.

Damp-proof course An impermeable layer put in exterior walls to prevent damp rising up the wall.

Damp-proof membrane An impermeable layer put in floors to prevent damp rising.

ACKNOWLEDGEMENTS

The publishers would like to thank Jan Eaton for devising and writing the Soft Furnishings section; Fiona Skrine for devising and demonstrating the special paint effects on pages 58-63; and Pat Murphy for demonstrating the carpet laying sequences on pages 134-7. Many thanks also to New Islington & Hackney Housing Association for the use of one of their properties that was awaiting repair. In addition, the publishers would like to thank the companies listed below for their generous help in either loaning or providing materials and equipment for use in the production of this title. For more details, see the Suppliers and Useful Addresses list.

J D Beardmore & Co Ltd
Black & Decker
Crown Paints
Fireplace Designers Ltd
Forbo Nairn Ltd
General Woodwork Supplies Ltd
Gripperrods plc
Hobbs & Co Ltd
Hodkin & Jones (Sheffield) Ltd
Ideal-Standard Ltd

H & R Johnson Tiles Ltd
Junckers Ltd
Kosset Carpets Ltd
Mosley-Stone
Oracstar Ltd
Plasplugs Ltd
Daniel Platt Ltd
Stanley Tools
Whincop & Son Ltd

The publishers would also like to thank the following companies for their kind permission to reproduce the following pictures in this book; they apologize for any unintentional omissions and will be happy to rectify this in future editions.

t = top; b = bottom; c = centre; l = left; r = right.

Addis Ltd: page 203 cl.
The Amtico Company Ltd: page 99 br.
Laura Ashley: pages 152 tl, 202 br, 182 t, 184 r, 187 br, 190 bl, 199 br.
Richard Burbidge Ltd: pages 20, 152-5, 194.
Castelnau Tiles: pages 98 br, 151 tr.
Concord Lighting Ltd: pages 24 b, 25 cl cr b, 29 tl b, 30 r, 31 bc br, 33 br.
Corres Mexican Tiles: page 96 cr.
Cliffhanger Shelving Systems: pages 202 tl, 203 tr.
Crown Paints: pages 36, 40 tr cr, 68-9, 69 cr br.
Cuprinol Ltd: pages 41 bl br, 125 b.
Dulux: pages 14, 16 b, 17 tl, 21 tr, 22 tl,

38, 39, 40 tl, 41 t, 150, 152 b, 185 br, 194 bl, 204 b, 213 t.
Cristal (H & R Johnson Tiles) Ltd: pages 18 b, 96 bl, 205 tr.
Crucial Trading Ltd: pages 123 b.
Fired Earth Tiles plc: pages 94, 96 tr, 97, 98 t bl.
Fireplace Designers Ltd: page 151 tl.
Forbo–CP (Fablon) Ltd: pages 16 t, 28, 66 b, 68 l, 69 bl, 153 b.
Forbo–Kingfisher Ltd: pages 18 t, 66 t, 67 t, 173 r, 195 tr.
Forbo–Nairn Ltd: pages 99 t, 123 tr, 124 t, 141.
Harlequin Wallcoverings Ltd: 21 tl, 64, 67 b, 152 b, 191 t, 192 br.
Harrison Drape: pages 21 b, 180 t, 181 t.
Hayloft Woodwork: pages 17 b, 204 t.
Heuga: pages 123 tl, 135 bl br.
Junckers Ltd: pages 19 b, 27 cr, 124 b, 125 t, 147, 211.
Kevin MacPartland: page 153 tr.
Mazda Lighting: pages 24 t, 25 t, 26, 27 tl tr cl, 29 tr, 30 l, 31 t bl, 32, 33 t.
The Merchant Tiler: page 114.
MFI: pages 17 tr, 19 t, 202 bl, 205 tl.
Monkwell Fabrics and Wallpapers: page 23 b.
Mr Tomkinson: pages 120, 122.
Philips Lighting Ltd: page 33 bl.
Sanderson: pages 22 tr b, 133 b, 186 t, 198 t.
Muriel Short Designs: page 193 br.
Silver Lynx Products: page 205 c.
Spur Shelving Ltd: pages 203 b, 205 b.
Today Interiors: pages 23 t, 174.
Wicanders: pages 99 cr, 124 c.
Elizabeth Whiting and Associates: page 189 br.